# A LIGHT IN THE DARKNESS:
Bible Study for Children and Teens

# A LIGHT IN THE DARKNESS:

## Bible Study for Children and Teens

Bethany Saros

OCABS PRESS
ST PAUL, MINNESOTA 55124
2020

A LIGHT IN THE DARKNESS:
BIBLE STUDY FOR CHILDREN AND TEENS


Copyright © 2020 by
Bethany Saros


ISBN 1-60191-048-7

PRINTED IN THE UNITED STATES OF AMERICA

A Light in the Darkness:
Bible Study for Children and Teens

ISBN 1-60191-048-7

Published by OCABS Press, St. Paul, Minnesota.
Printed in the United States of America.

Books are available through OCABS Press at special discounts for bulk purchases in the United States by academic institutions, churches, and other organizations. For more information please email OCABS Press at press@ocabs.org.

*For Sarah*

# Foreword

In *Torah to the Gentiles*, I challenged my readers to dismiss church school curricula in favor of studying the primary text of Scripture. Our children, I explained, are capable of learning difficult or complex stories, if only parents and other adults are willing to make an effort. Bethany took this challenge seriously. Her book, *A Light in the Darkness*, illumines the path for any parent who feels unprepared or ill-qualified to teach Scripture to children.

Through her faithful study of Scripture, Bethany shows how any layperson with the ability to read can teach children—even as the adults themselves are learning—while avoiding the pitfalls of interpretation and theological speculation. Teaching, she explains, is as simple as defining words, following the plot, identifying characters, looking up historical facts, and, most importantly, sticking to the text. Parents should read the stories of the Bible to their children without comment. "Narration," Bethany explains, "teaches children submission to the story." I hasten to add that her book challenges parents to do the same. That Bethany takes this directive seriously is evident in her insightful exegesis of various passages.

I am thankful to God for the seed of his teaching at work in Bethany's wonderful book. Her commitment to biblical education, working shoulder-to-shoulder with other parents, has helped to deepen our church school program's focus on the study of the biblical text. Most recently, this focus led to a community-wide youth project to memorize the full text of St. Paul's letter to the Galatians. Not to understand or interpret, but to learn the content of Galatians. In these worrisome times, it is Bethany's hope, and mine, that the wisdom of St. Paul's magisterial epistle—committed to memory—will be a light in the darkness for all our children.

Fr. Marc Boulos

# A Note About Narration

My first day of teaching the Bible to a multi-age Sunday School class was an abject failure. Not only did I have no idea what I was doing, I felt woefully ill-equipped. I spoke to other parents in my parish who were also scheduled to teach and we all shared the same opinion—we had no idea what we were doing and we felt unqualified to teach. The kids were bored and asking in the car on the way home what was the point of going to Sunday School? Expecting them to retain anything seemed ridiculous. I began searching for the perfect curriculum to fix the problem.

The more I looked, the more I noticed a glaring hole in the available literature. There were books about fasting, books about journeys of converts to the Orthodox Church, books about bringing children to church, stories of saints for children; but there was nothing about teaching the Bible to children. The "children's Bibles" seemed insulting to their intelligence and I did not like the idea of someone else interpreting the Bible for my kids. It is said that if you don't see the book you want, *write the book*. So, I did.

As I began this effort, I wasn't completely confident how to go about it. I took passages from the Bible and started asking a short series of specific questions. It was only after

I started homeschooling my three kids that I learned that the structure I was creating had a name: narration.

Narration is an excellent technique used for calling children's attention to the text. In the early elementary years, children are taught by hearing a story read aloud and then answering a series of questions related to the text. The goal is to keep the focus on the storyline and the words—rather than allowing for free interpretation and an emotional response. This lays the groundwork for teaching children how to order their thoughts so that in later years, they can begin to summarize passages in their own words. What today's children appear to struggle with in writing is the inability to articulate their thoughts. Susan Wise Bauer puts it this way in her book *Writing with Ease: Strong Fundamentals:*

> *"Imagine that you've had a year or so of conversational French, taught in a traditional way out of a textbook, with practice in speaking twice a week or so. After that first year, your teacher asks you to explain the problem of evil in French. You're likely to experience brain freeze...a halting and incoherent attempt to express complicated ideas in a medium which is unfamiliar...Rather the conventions of the French language need to become second nature, automatic...so that you can concentrate on the ideas, rather than on the medium used to express them."*

While this is not a book about writing, it is a book that draws on principles essential to writing. It teaches children to order their thoughts and rely on the text for information so that they can put it down on paper. The purpose of studying the Bible is not for one's own gratification—it is so that it can be taught to others. Narration teaches children *submission* to the story—which is critical when studying the Bible. You cannot bounce around from here to there—the *order* is important to understanding how the Bible functions.

Before a student can learn to write, he/she needs to learn to narrate. Narration is simply taking a passage and putting it into their own words. The educator assists this process by asking a series of questions relating directly to the passage. Susan Wise Bauer insists on having children respond in *complete sentences*. This is essential because when they are older, they will be required to summarize passages in answer to the more general question: what happened? Never is the child asked for their opinion or their emotional response. Narration forces the child to deal with facts—it is a logical approach to literary discussion and to life.

For some older children, it may be necessary to start with the simple, specific questions. Some of them may not be familiar with narration and therefore they may need to start at the beginning. This is completely fine. The Bible does not require a Ph.D. in order to be understood but some fundamental skills are required. Children and adults can work together to learn these basics.

Following the example of Susan Wise Bauer, I have tried
to structure the questions about the Biblical passages in a
similar fashion to her books "Writing with Ease".
However, I have included some of my own commentary
and analysis to offer examples to the educator of what
providing context for children may look like. This is not
intended to be a curriculum nor should it be used as such.
It is my hope that parents and educators who feel
overwhelmed by the Biblical text will find inspiration
from these pages to continue or perhaps even begin their
study of the teaching.

# Contents

Foreword   9

*A Note About Narration*   11

*Contents*   15

*Introduction*   17

**Chapter 1: Matthew 2**   **21**
Lesson: Matthew 2:1-6   22
Lesson: Matthew 2:7-12   25
Lesson: Matthew 2:13-18   27
Lesson: Matthew 2:19-23   28

**Chapter 2: Matthew 7-8**   **31**
Lesson: Matthew 7:24-28; 8:1-4   31
*Miracles In the Old Testament*   34
Lesson: Matthew 8:5-13   37
Lesson: Matthew 8:14-22   40
Lesson: Matthew 8:23-27   43
Lesson: Matthew 8:28-34   44

**Chapter 3: Matthew 18**   **49**
Lesson: Matthew 18:1-6   49
Lesson: Matthew 18:7-9   52
Lesson: Matthew 18:10-14   53
Lesson: Matthew 18:15-20   55
Lesson: Matthew 18:21-35   58

**Chapter 4: Matthew 25**   **61**
Lesson: Matthew 25:1-13   61
Lesson: Matthew 25:14-30   64
Lesson: Matthew 25:31-46   68

**Chapter 5: The Pauline Epistles**   **73**

Lesson: 1 Corinthians 13:1-3                                74
Lesson: 1 Corinthians 13:4-7                                76
Lesson: 1 Corinthians 13:8-13                               78
Lesson: Galatians 4:1-7                                     81
Lesson: Galatians 4:8-20                                    82
Lesson: Galatians 4:21-31                                   85

*Chapter 6: Matthew 26-28*                                  *89*
Lesson: Matthew 26:1-16                                     89
Lesson: Matthew 26:20-25                                    94
Lesson: Matthew 26:26-35                                    96
Lesson: Matthew 26:47-56                                    98
Lesson: Matthew 26:47-56                                    101
Lesson: Matthew 26:57-68                                    105
Lesson: Matthew 26:69-75                                    107
Lesson: Matthew 27:1-10                                     110
Lesson: Matthew 27: 11-14                                   112
Lesson: Matthew 27: 15-26                                   114
Lesson: Matthew 27:27-37                                    117
Lesson: Matthew 27:38-66                                    119
Lesson: Matthew 27:45-50                                    121
Lesson: Matthew 27:51-61                                    122
Lesson: Matthew 27:62-66                                    125
Lesson: Matthew 28:1-15                                     126
Lesson: Matthew 28:11-15                                    128
Lesson: Matthew 28:16-20                                    129

*Epilogue: On Parenting*                                    *133*

*Helpful Resources*                                         *139*
The Ephesus School Podcast Network                          139
Other Sources                                               140

# Introduction

If you step into an Eastern Orthodox Sunday School class, it is very likely that you will hear little actual Bible study. Speaking to my own experience, we spent a great deal more time on church history and traditions than we did on actual Scripture. At the time of this writing, the Greek Orthodox archdiocese offers an outline, "Living Our Orthodox Faith", for church school educators on their website—what each grade should know at the end of the school year. The first-grade class is titled "Me and My World" and the first unit is "About Me". First graders learn that they are special and unique, and God has a wonderful plan for their lives. It's all very optimistic. As my friend Sarah once said, "God loves you and has a wonderful plan for your life. Sometimes that plan includes being eaten by lions." An inconvenient truth often ignored by church school educators, parents, and even priests.

As the children grow older, they are exposed to more history and tradition. The emphasis is always on the rules and loving one's neighbor is mentioned in passing—it is not the central teaching for Sunday School. For example, knowing that the Ascension of Christ comes forty days after the Resurrection is listed as something they should know from church school—rather than something learned by participating in liturgy. As far as the Bible is concerned, it is mentioned that Scripture was written by people inspired by God and that we are to live and follow its message…but there is no concrete discussion of what that message *is* and there are simply more lists of rules and traditions to follow. With such an unsatisfying overview of history and lack of challenging material for children, is it any wonder that the Orthodox Church struggles to retain its youth?

That is not to say that rules and traditions are negative— in fact, they can be very positive. But rules and traditions are best conveyed through participation in community life and liturgical services—another thing that I have seen some Orthodox churches move away from. The children all disappear after communion to Sunday School or are scowled at by church members who believe that children should be seen and not heard, or (my least favorite) hustled off to a cry room or a nursery at the first sign of natural child behavior. We outsource their spiritual education to Sunday School teachers and settle in to relax. Someone else is teaching our kids—which is fine with us because we believe that we are inadequately prepared to do so ourselves. Then we believe that a one-hour class once a week is sufficient to keep children interested in church. As parents, we should be encouraging our children to participate in liturgy and church life while also reading Scripture to them every day at home— engaging and challenging them to love wisdom instead of money and consumerism.

One of my biggest challenges with teaching Scripture to my own three children has been my confidence. I have often felt that I am not qualified to teach the Bible...mostly because I also find it difficult to understand. However, I have learned that one does not need to have all the answers in order to teach children—learning *together* is the important thing. A parent does not need to embody wisdom in order to teach it—what we need to pass on to our children is a *love* of wisdom. Our job as parents is not to teach our children *what* to think. Our mission should be to teach the love of wisdom by pursuing it with them, so that we as parents can grow with our children in knowledge and faith. This feels counterintuitive to what education looks like today: all-knowing teachers saving students from ignorance with their ideology *du jour*. The problem with this method is that it allows the teacher to impose his agenda upon the pupil who doesn't know any better. Instead of learning critical thinking and studying the actual text, the student walks away believing that his opinion (or the teacher's) is the only thing that matters—the text is simply a conversational point and it's only interpretation that counts. This relationship is detrimental to both teacher and student. While respect and deference toward the teacher's station, knowledge, and experience must be established among the students, the educator must also be open to learning alongside the class—*not from the students*—but *from the text* itself. From this perspective, the idea of learning with the learners should come as a relief.

That is the goal of this book. I hope to offer parents and spiritual educators not an outline of *what* to think when studying the Bible, but a demonstration of *how* to study the Bible. This is not a book about my personal opinions, but rather, a guide on how to study the Bible as literature with children. My objective is to help teachers present the content of the Bible to their students without imposing an interpretation. When I first began to study the Bible this way, the message clicked, "stick to the text," —something my toughest English professor used to say. "Your opinion doesn't matter…what does the text say?" If you had anything to say at all, you had to be prepared to back it up with a text. That is what studying the Bible as literature looks like. You are not infusing your opinions into Scripture, rather, you are looking at the actual text and asking, "What is it saying? What does it mean?" The answers may surprise you. *Stick to the text.*

# Chapter 1: Matthew 2

W e'll start with a story that everyone knows. The lectionary for the Nativity of Christ appoints Matthew 2:1-12 as the Gospel reading. While it may be easier to explain the shorter reading for children (depending on what ages you are dealing with), as an educator, it is important to take a step back from the lectionary to consider the assigned reading in context of the entire chapter. It is also important to approach the story with a book club mentality. You are not there to offer children the story through your own lens…you are there to present the story to them as is and to guide them as they begin to pay attention and consider it for themselves. To this end, narration is a useful tool.

Any time you make sure children are paying attention by asking questions about what they just, you are engaged in narration. You can do this on the fly while reading out loud but it can be helpful for you as the educator to take some time to prepare beforehand. The questions themselves should refer the child back to the text. This alone may be sufficient depending on the age and attention span of the group. If you do some research, you can also present scientific and historical data to provide deeper context for the class as they grapple with the text's meaning. This book offers examples to guide you so that you will be ready for your next class or study with your own children. Then you will feel more prepared instead of intimidated. Remember, your goal is to present the story as is. Children will make their own connections in ways that may surprise you.

For example, in Sunday School at our church, one of our teachers was reading to the children the story of Peter's refusal to eat food given to him by God that was considered "common" (Acts 10). As the children listened, one of them colored a picture of Noah's ark, which had been loaded up with clean and unclean animals mixed together. Since the entire point of Acts 10 was about Jews and Gentiles intermingling—that no man is "common or unclean"—the teacher was excited that the child had made this connection without any outside guidance. Children do not need your filter—they need the text presented to them. God will do the rest.

## Lesson: Matthew 2:1-6

*"Now when Jesus was born in Bethlehem of Judea, in the days of Herod the king, behold, wise men from the East came to Jerusalem, saying, 'Where is he who has been born king of the Jews? For we have seen his star in the East, and have come to worship him.' When Herod the king heard this, he was troubled, and all Jerusalem with him; and assembling all the chief priests and scribes of the people, he inquired of them where the Christ was to be born. They told him, 'In Bethlehem of Judea; for so it is written by the prophet: And you, O Bethlehem, in the land of Judah, are by no*

*means least among the rulers of Judah; for from you
shall come a ruler who will govern my people Israel.'"
(Matthew 2:1-6)*

Have older children take turns reading the passage aloud
in order to keep them engaged. Younger children may
enjoy drawing pictures of what is happening in the
story—the wise men, the star, King Herod, etc.

Questions to ask as you go along:

- Where are the wise men from and who are
  they looking for?

- What do they plan to do when they find the
  king of the Jews?

- How did they know that Jesus had been
  born?

- Where does Herod live?

- What does Herod think about the wise
  men's mission? Is he happy?

- Why would Herod be troubled or upset
  about someone being born king of the Jews?

- Why is it important that Jesus is born in
  Bethlehem?

By asking book club type questions, the adult is not
imposing their views but keeping the focus on the story
itself and the characters. Facilitating discussion, sharing

empirical knowledge, and provoking insight are the ultimate goal.

## Discussion

Young children who are listening to this passage might be interested in the star. You may talk about ancient astronomers and how they studied the stars in order to make sense of the world. According to *The Cambridge Illustrated History of Astronomy*, ancient astronomy had two goals: to demonstrate that the movements of the planets were predictable and to accurately predict these movements. Even then, making sense of the universe was important. Babylonian astronomers studied the heavens in order to keep an eye on the cycles of the moon as well as unusual events in "every aspect of nature". Their observations were not limited to only the sky. Egyptian astronomers studied the stars and created a calendar based on their conclusions, while Greek astronomers were more interested in the relationship of the heavens to the earth. Chinese astronomers believed that anything out of the ordinary in the sky meant disaster and that the government was not ruling like it should—an interesting fact in light of the tension between Herod and Jesus. An unusual star would definitely catch the attention of anyone studying the sky.

Bethlehem is mentioned several times throughout the passage. Why is it important that Jesus was born in this particular place? From an historical perspective, King

David—an ancestor of Joseph, Jesus' earthly father—was born there. It is also prophesied in Micah 5:2 that a ruler in Israel will be born in Bethlehem:

*"But you, O Bethlehem Eph'rathah, who are little to be among the clans of Judah, from you shall come forth for me one who is to be ruler in Israel, whose origin is from of old, from ancient days."*

The word *Bethlehem* means "house of bread". Children can draw a picture of what they think this looks like. Talk about how bread—an ancient staple food—is a source of life for human beings. Use practical examples like the American expression, "bread and water." Challenge your students, "why are bread and water essential for life?"

## Lesson: Matthew 2:7-12

*"Then Herod summoned the wise men secretly and ascertained from them what time the star appeared; and he sent them to Bethlehem, saying, 'Go and search diligently for the child, and when you have found him bring me word, that I too may come and worship him.' When they had heard the king they went their way; and lo, the star which they had seen in the East went before them, till it came to rest over the place where the child was. When they saw the star, they rejoiced exceedingly with great joy; and going into the house they saw the child with Mary his mother, and they fell down and worshiped him. Then, opening their treasures, they offered him gifts, gold and*

*frankincense and myrrh. And being warned in a dream not to return to Herod, they departed to their own country by another way." (Matthew 2:7-12)*

- Why would Herod summon the wise men in secret?

- What did he tell the wise men when he sent them to Bethlehem?

- Does he really want to worship Jesus?

- What kind of gifts did the wise men bring Jesus?

- Why would they give him those things instead of toys?

- Did the wise men go back to tell Herod about Jesus? Why not?

## Discussion

Some of the answers to these questions might require a little preparation beforehand from the adult. However, if you don't have time to prepare, it is perfectly acceptable to look up something on a phone or a computer or whatever is immediately available. It is okay to not have an answer ready. This way, the adult is learning alongside the children, which can also have significant impact. Having all of the answers is not the goal. The goal is to learn and to pass along the content of the Bible.

## Lesson: Matthew 2:13-18

*"Now when they had departed, behold, an angel of the Lord appeared to Joseph in a dream and said, 'Rise, take the child and his mother and flee to Egypt, and remain there till I tell you; for Herod is about to search for the child, to destroy him.' And he rose and took the child and his mother by night, and departed to Egypt, and remained there until the death of Herod. This was to fulfil what the Lord had spoken by the prophet, 'Out of Egypt have I called my son.' Then Herod, when he saw that he had been tricked by the wise men, was in a furious rage, and he sent and killed all the male children in Bethlehem and in all that region who were two years old or under, according to the time which he had ascertained from the wise men. Then was fulfilled what was spoken by the prophet Jeremiah: 'A voice was heard in Ramah, wailing and loud lamentation, Rachel weeping for her children; she refused to be consoled, because they were no more.'" (Matthew 2:13-18)*

- Who told Joseph that Herod was coming?

- Where did Joseph, Mary, and Jesus go?

- What did Herod do after he found out that the wise men had tricked him?

## *Discussion*

There may be hesitance on the part of some adults to read this part of the story to children, and understandably so. Violence is a crucial part of the story of Jesus—from beginning to end. In *The Fellowship of the Ring*, Galadrial gives Frodo a vial that contains the light of the Eärendil. She tells him, "Let it be a light to you in dark places." Galadrial knows that Frodo is in for a dark journey, but she doesn't tell him in which situation to use the starlight. She simply gives it to him, tells him what it is for, and lets him make the decision on when to use it. Life can be a dark journey. Let us give our children the Bible as their light in dark places but let them decide when and how to use it.

Suffering is a part of our world. As Neil Gaiman (paraphrasing G.K. Chesterton) says, "Fairytales tell us that the dragon can be beaten." This is not to suggest that the Bible should be treated as a collection of fairytales, however, fairytales, like the Bible, are literature, written to convey meaning. We need only trust our children's ability to hear and learn from these stories.

## Lesson: Matthew 2:19-23

*"But when Herod died, behold, an angel of the Lord appeared in a dream to Joseph in Egypt, saying, 'Rise, take the child and his mother, and go to the land of Israel, for those who sought the child's life are dead.'*

*And he rose and took the child and his mother, and went to the land of Israel. But when he heard that Archela'us reigned over Judea in place of his father Herod, he was afraid to go there, and being warned in a dream he withdrew to the district of Galilee. And he went and dwelt in a city called Nazareth, that what was spoken by the prophets might be fulfilled, 'He shall be called a Nazarene.'" (Matthew 2:19-23)*

- Who told Joseph that Herod was dead?

- Where did Joseph, Mary, and Jesus go?

- Why was Joseph afraid to go to Judea?

- Where did he take Mary and Jesus instead?

## Discussion

As you can see, academic knowledge and special qualifications are not necessary to teach children the Bible. Anyone can sit down and examine the text and come up with a list of questions to ask children in Sunday School. Our job as adults is to present Scripture to children—not to interpret it for them.

# Chapter 2: Matthew 7-8

The stories found in the gospels are readily accessible to children—Jesus is always going somewhere and doing something—which makes it easy for kids to follow. Nevertheless, when we encounter certain elements, like the miracles of Jesus, it can be more challenging. It's tempting to infuse our own interpretations—what we *think* the text means or how it makes us *feel*—but what we *think* and how we *feel* is irrelevant. As our priest reminds our parish every week, feelings can help motivate us to act on the Bible's imperative, but they can also work against it. Either way, our duty is to follow the commandments of God. Our feelings and thoughts have no bearing on the meaning of the author's story or our duty to submit to it. No matter what we feel, we are accountable to the Bible's objective content. As a parent and an educator, you must work through your own emotional responses and not confuse them with the data. *Stick to the text.*

## Lesson: Matthew 7:24-28; 8:1-4

*"Every one then who hears these words of mine and does them will be like a wise man who built his house upon the rock; and the rain fell, and the floods came, and the winds blew and beat upon that house, but it*

*did not fall, because it had been founded on the rock.
And every one who hears these words of mine and
does not do them will be like a foolish man who built
his house upon the sand; and the rain fell, and the
floods came, and the winds blew and beat against
that house, and it fell; and great was the fall of it.'
And when Jesus finished these sayings, the crowds
were astonished at his teaching, for he taught them as
one who had authority, and not as their scribes.*

*"When he came down from the mountain, great
crowds followed him; and behold, a leper came to him
and knelt before him, saying, 'Lord, if you will, you
can make me clean.' And he stretched out his hand and
touched him saying, 'I will; be clean.' And
immediately his leprosy was cleansed. And Jesus said
to him, 'See that you say nothing to any one; but go,
show yourself to the priest, and offer the gift that
Moses commanded for a proof to the people.'"*
*(Matthew 7:24-28, 8:1-4)*

- What is the definition of amazed?

- Why are the crowds amazed?

- Why are the crowds following Jesus?

- What is leprosy?

- What does the man say to Jesus?

- Does Jesus heal him?

- What does Jesus tell the man to do after he heals him?

## Discussion

In many interpretations of the gospels, the crowds are depicted as an object of sympathy. However, in the Gospel of Mark, Jesus always tries to escape the crowds because he knows that all they want is to see a miracle—they don't care about the biblical teaching or his mission[1]. Here, in Matthew, Jesus is demonstrating that he is not here to change the law but to lead the people back to the correct application of it. Discuss what it means to be amazed. Kids are often impressed by the wrong thing—name brand clothing, big houses, money—making it easy for them to be led astray by someone who wants to hurt them. The object of a person's amazement demonstrates their priorities. Note that correct priorities are demonstrated in the story of the centurion, found in the subsequent passage of Matthew.

Talk about leprosy in medical and historical terms. Also known as Hansen's Disease, leprosy is a bacterial ailment that affects the nerves, skin, eyes, and nose. It was previously thought that leprosy was contagious but we now know this is incorrect. If caught early enough, it can even be cured. Explain that people with leprosy are often ostracized from society, even today. For example, there is

---

[1] Boulos, Marc. Benton, Richard. The Bible as Literature Podcast, "Episode 168: This People Honors Me With Their Lips," ephesusschool.org/this-people-honors-me-with-their-lips/.

a leper colony in Hawaii, Kalaupapa, where people have been living since 1860. Over 8,000 people died there. Although the quarantine was lifted in 1969, six patients voluntarily remain. Their stories of abandonment and stigmatization are heartbreaking. Parents left children at the colony. Children were separated from sick parents—never to see them again. Entire bloodlines were erased so that no one would know that these children were related to someone with the disease. Leprosy has a long history of isolation and devastation. This is why it is important to follow the text and to share general knowledge without imposing our interpretations. Do not try to describe leprosy as a depiction of the man's spiritual state. In the story, it is those who are free from disease who are truly sick, because they exclude the leper from their community. Children need facts, not personal conjecture.

## Miracles In the Old Testament

In the passage above, Jesus is teaching in Galilee—his home turf. We know from Matthew and other gospels that Jesus is not accepted in his hometown (Matthew 12; Luke 4:20-29). Matthew demonstrates how the outsider becomes like Jesus in the passages about the leper and the centurion.

Jesus is also testing the people. He wants them to cling to his Father's teaching and not to follow after signs and wonders. That is why he keeps the man's healing a secret, so as not to indulge the throng of people who don't really believe in his teaching:

> *"If a prophet arises among you, or a dreamer of dreams, and gives you a sign or a wonder, and the sign or wonder which he tells you comes to pass, and if he says, 'Let us go after other gods,' which you have not known, 'and let us serve them,' you shall not listen to the words of that prophet or to that dreamer of dreams; for the Lord your God is testing you, to know whether you love the Lord your God with all your heart and with all your soul. You shall walk after the Lord your God and fear him, and keep his commandments and obey his voice, and you shall serve him and cleave to him." (Deuteronomy 13:1-4)*

In order to remain consistent with the teaching of the Law, Jesus sends the healed man to see the priest. Leviticus 13 clearly requires lepers to be examined by the priest before they can be declared clean. When preaching on this passage, my priest often reminds us that this instruction pushes the priest to care for the leper, making every effort to reintegrate him into the community, even if it means risking the priest's health:

> *[1] Then the Lord spoke to Moses and to Aaron, saying, [2] "When a man has on the skin of his body a swelling or a scab or a bright spot, and it becomes an infection of leprosy on the skin of his body, then he shall be brought to Aaron the priest or to one of his sons the priests. [3] The priest shall look at the mark on the skin of the body, and if the hair in the infection has turned white and the*

*infection appears to be deeper than the skin of his body, it is an infection of leprosy; when the priest has looked at him, he shall pronounce him unclean. 4 But if the bright spot is white on the skin of his body, and it does not appear to be deeper than the skin, and the hair on it has not turned white, then the priest shall isolate him who has the infection for seven days. 5 The priest shall look at him on the seventh day, and if in his eyes the infection has not changed and the infection has not spread on the skin, then the priest shall isolate him for seven more days. 6 The priest shall look at him again on the seventh day, and if the infection has faded and the mark has not spread on the skin, then the priest shall pronounce him clean; it is only a scab. And he shall wash his clothes and be clean.*

*7 "But if the scab spreads farther on the skin after he has shown himself to the priest for his cleansing, he shall appear again to the priest. 8 The priest shall look, and if the scab has spread on the skin, then the priest shall pronounce him unclean; it is leprosy.*

*9 "When the infection of leprosy is on a man, then he shall be brought to the priest. 10 The priest shall then look, and if there is a white swelling in the skin, and it has turned the hair white, and there is quick raw flesh in the swelling, 11 it is a chronic leprosy on the skin of his body, and the priest shall pronounce him unclean; he shall not isolate him, for he is unclean. 12 If the leprosy breaks out farther on the skin, and the leprosy covers all the skin of him who has the infection from his head even to his feet, as far as the priest can see, [13] then the priest shall look, and behold, if the leprosy has covered all his body, he shall pronounce clean him who has the infection; it has all turned white and he is clean. (Leviticus 13: 1-13)*

Talk to the children about how it feels to be excluded from a group. Has anyone at school ever been ostracized from a group or social activity? Why were they put outside? What risks, if any, have your students taken to help them?

## Lesson: Matthew 8:5-13

*"As he entered Caper'na-um, a centurion came forward to him, beseeching him and saying, 'Lord, my servant is lying paralyzed at home, in terrible distress.' And he said to him, 'I will come and heal him.' But the centurion answered him, 'Lord, I am not worthy to have you come under my roof; but only say the word, and my servant will be healed. For I am a man under authority, with soldiers under me; and I say to one, 'Go' and he goes, and to another 'Come,' and he comes, and to my slave, 'Do this,' and he does it.' When Jesus heard him, he marveled, and said to those who followed him, 'Truly, I say to you, not even in Israel have I found such faith. I tell you, many will come from east and west and sit at table with Abraham, Isaac, and Jacob in the kingdom of heaven, while the sons of the kingdom will be thrown into the outer darkness; there men will weep and gnash their teeth.' And to the centurion Jesus said, 'Go; be it done*

*for you as you have believed.' And the servant was
healed at that very moment." (Matthew 8:5-13)*

- What is the name of the town Jesus entered?

- What does Caper'na-um mean?

- What does the word "centurion" mean?

- What does the word "authority" mean?

- What does the word "believe" or *"pistevo"*
  (Greek) mean?

- Who did the centurion want Jesus to heal?

- What did the centurion say when Jesus
  offered to come with him to heal his
  servant?

## Discussion

It is notable here in Matthew that Jesus's second miracle
is for a Gentile centurion. The message is clear: even a
Roman centurion understands the teaching better than
the Pharisees. Soldiers have correct priorities and
understand the chain of command. In this passage, the
centurion believes in Jesus but the word *believe* in English
is a misreading of the Greek word *pistevo*. It does not
mean "believe" as in "I believe in feminism" or "I believe
in conservatism". *Pistevo* means "trust" —like the way
soldiers trust their battle buddy to have their back in a
foxhole. The centurion does not need Jesus to come to his

house to heal his servant because he trusts the command of Jesus—*he knows that Jesus has his back.* Unlike the crowds of people who have grown up in the synagogue, he trusts the authority of the teaching of Jesus. The Gentile, or the outsider, has trust (faith) that his servant will be healed whether Jesus is present or not. This miracle is an important example not only of trust but of inclusion of the outsider. Gentiles are not excluded from table fellowship with Christ. Talk to children about examples of inclusion and trust in their own lives.

The word "authority" is a word that gets modern day people up in arms. Nobody likes authority—rebellion against it is encouraged and celebrated in today's world. In Greek, *authority* is understood as "the power to act"--*exousia.* While the English dictionary holds a similar definition, it is also defined as a person or an organization having corporate or political power—which is how most modern-day Christians think of authority. So, when Jesus says "authority" in the Bible, it is easy to assume that he is claiming to be the man in charge. But Jesus is not the final authority—he merely has the power to act because the Father—the ultimate power—has delegated his authority through the content of the biblical teaching. If I tell my son to inform his sister that she is permitted to watch TV, this does not mean that my son has the authority to grant this permission. He carries my authority, but it does not belong to him—he is just a messenger. The same is true of Jesus is in the New Testament.

## Lesson: Matthew 8:14-22

*"And when Jesus entered Peter's house, he saw his mother-in-law lying sick with a fever; he touched her hand, and the fever left her, and she rose and served him. That evening they brought to him many who were possessed with demons; and he cast out the spirits with a word, and healed all who were sick. This was to fulfill what was spoken by the prophet Isaiah, 'He took our infirmities and bore our diseases.'*

*"Now when Jesus saw great crowds around him, he gave orders to go over to the other side. And a scribe came up and said to him, 'Teacher, I will follow you wherever you go.' And Jesus said to him, 'Foxes have holes, and the birds of the air have nests; but the Son of man has nowhere to lay his head.' Another of the disciples said to him, 'Lord, let me first go and bury my father.' But Jesus said to him, 'Follow me, and leave the dead to bury their own dead.'"* (Matthew 8:14-22)

- Who did Jesus heal in this passage?

- Which prophet said that God would "take our infirmities and bear our diseases"?

- Why did Jesus say that the "Son of man has nowhere to lay his head" when the scribe wanted to go with him?

- When a disciple wanted to go and bury his father, Jesus told him to let the "dead bury their own dead".

## Discussion

A common mistake when reading this passage is to assume that the prophecy of Isaiah predicts the birth Jesus. Again, we as teachers must be careful to separate opinion from fact. The prophets do not predict the future—instead, their stories were written to expose the people's disobedience during their lifetime, and to announce that God's judgment would bring an end to the social order of their day. To understand this context, take a moment to read Isaiah 53 with your class. The prophets may feel abstract to children, but it is important that they become familiar with these parts of the Bible.

When Jesus gets into the boat to go over to "the other side", according to Fr. Paul Tarazi, this is to indicate his movement away from Jerusalem and towards Rome, emphasizing that Jesus' true followers understand the perspective of the gospel: there is no difference between Jew and Gentile.[2]

It may seem strange that Jesus is turning away people who want to go with him. In the gospel of Mark, when the Scribe says that he will follow him, Jesus gives it to him straight: everyone *but* the Son of man has a place in

---

[2] Paul Nadim Tarazi, *The New Testament: Introduction, vol. 4, Matthew and the Canon*, (St. Paul, Minnesota: OCABS Press, 2009).

society. Not only is Jesus homeless, but he has been rejected by his blood relatives, the people of Israel. "Leave the dead to bury their own dead," Jesus commands, because human seed will pass away, but God's seed—the seed that produced Jesus—will never die. In the Bible, family and tribe have nothing to do with bloodline. The gospel of Matthew emphasizes that Jesus' family are all those who gather together to hear and follow his teaching. A child who may have been rejected by biological parents becomes part of a family through adoption. Where our culture values *appearances*, the Bible values *behavior*. A child is not a son or daughter because they look like their parent, but because they behave in a way the reflects their parents' teaching. Talk to the children about the problem of racism: judging or even excluding a person based on appearances.

There is another aspect to Jesus' warning about burying the dead. When the disciple wants to bury his father, he is delaying and making excuses, putting his bloodline ahead of his duty to the Lord's teaching. "I can't come right now, Jesus, I have to go bury my father." We see excuses like these in the passage about the wedding feast, when the invitees continually come up with reasons why they can't attend the party. Parents are familiar with these kinds of excuses. When they tell a child to clean his or her room, the child responds, "Okay, Mama, I'll do it, but first..." Jesus wants us to drop everything and follow him...immediately. The disciple is stalling. Ask the children how they respond when their parents ask them to do something important.

## Lesson: Matthew 8:23-27

*"And when he got into the boat, his disciples followed him. And behold, there arose a great storm on the sea, so that the boat was being swamped by the waves; but he was asleep. And they went and woke him, saying, 'Save, Lord; we are perishing.' And he said to them, 'Why are you afraid, O men of little faith?' Then he rose and rebuked the winds and the sea; and there was a great calm. And the men marveled, saying, 'What sort of man is this, that even winds and sea obey him?'" (Matthew 8:23-27)*

- Why were the disciples so afraid?

- Are there similar stories elsewhere in the Bible? (Jonah)

- What did Jesus say to them when they woke him?

- Why didn't they trust Jesus? (because storms are scary and water is VERY scary— good discussion topic with kids)

- What did the men say after Jesus calmed the storm?

## *Discussion*

So far in this chapter, Jesus has healed a leper in the presence of people and a servant from afar. The storm is raging and he's asleep, which suggests that Jesus believes there is nothing to worry about. But the disciples are still afraid. Even after everything they've seen, they still don't get it, which is why Jesus says to them, "Why are you afraid?" Why *are* they afraid? Why do they lack trust? The Father of Jesus is in control, so Jesus isn't concerned and they shouldn't be worried either. Discuss with the children why worrying is a fruitless endeavor. Talk about how God is in control and how faith/trust in his teaching, no matter what happens to us, is essential. Remember what my friend Sarah said, "God loves you and has a wonderful plan for your life. Sometimes that plan includes being eaten by lions."

It's okay to be afraid. But if someone is so afraid that they can't trust God, then the fear becomes their god. Storms and water are scary. Reading the story of Jonah would be a good example of what happens when fear becomes the focus instead of trusting in the commandment.

## Lesson: Matthew 8:28-34

*"And when he came to the other side, to the country of the Gadarenes, two demoniacs met him, coming out of the tombs, so fierce that no one could pass that way. And behold, they cried out, 'What have you to*

*do with us, O Son of God? Have you come here to torment us before the time?' Now a herd of many swine was feeding at some distance from them. And the demons begged him, 'If you cast us out, send us away into the herd of swine.' And he said to them, 'Go.' So they came out and went into the swine; and behold, the whole herd rushed down the steep bank into the sea, and perished in the waters. The herdsmen fled, and going into the city they told everything, and what had happened to the demoniacs. And behold, all the city came out to meet Jesus; and when they saw him, they begged him to leave their neighborhood."* (Matthew 8:28-34)

- What is a demoniac?

- What did they say to Jesus?

- Where did they ask Jesus to send them?

- What are swine?

- What does the Law in the Old Testament say about swine?

- What happened to the herd after Jesus agreed to the demoniacs' request?

- What did the people of the city ask Jesus to do after they heard about the herd?

## Discussion

Look up the word "demoniac". It's not a word often used today and children may not know what it means. *Merriam Webster* defines "demoniac" as a "person possessed or influenced by a demon". Some children may want to know what a demon is. It is important not to scare them with tales of horned and winged creatures flying about with intentions to spiritually torment us. That is a good example of adults imposing their interpretation of the story on their students. Kids have enough to worry about in life without grown-ups terrifying them with human stories about demons and the Devil. In God's story, *the story of the Bible*, demons represent false teaching. In the Gospel of John, Jesus refers to the Devil as the "Father of Lies." (John 8:44) Until the two men in the story met Jesus, no other teacher was able to help them. Talk about the importance of telling the truth and of teaching and sharing knowledge with others.

It is also important to note that the two men are Gadarenes—Gentiles. The fact that Jesus healed them continues Matthew's emphasis on inclusion.

Explain to children that spending time thinking about yourself or putting yourself above others is demonic because it contradicts the teaching of Jesus...which is to love your neighbor and to consider the needs of others before yourself. Give some examples of modern teachings that contradict this message—"love yourself", "you are special", "you are unique", "follow your heart", etc.

Children today are brought up to prioritize themselves over others: *others* do not matter in our own pursuit of happiness. How many times have we heard someone say, "all I want is for my kids to be happy." God wants more. Much more.

Self-love is destructive and definitely not scriptural. The saying, "You are not the boss of me" best reflects the meaning of demon possession in the Bible, because it goes against the teaching of submission to one's neighbor and rejects the authority of God's teaching. The Lord Jesus Christ was not the boss of himself, so how dare we allow our children to speak this way? Sadly, in today's society, submission is a word that breeds contempt.

After the healing has taken place and the townspeople have come out to see for themselves, they "[beg] Jesus to leave their neighborhood". Why would they ask Jesus to leave after such a miracle? At first glance, it seems as though they are afraid of Jesus. It may surprise the children to know that the opposite is true. They are not afraid of Jesus. They are so thrilled by the miracle that they want to share it with everyone. Consider the previous passages where people have tried to keep Jesus for themselves.

Using the content of the biblical text, general knowledge, and literary context to train our children as critical thinkers is essential in the modern world. Children need to *know the facts* of the Bible—the actual content and meaning of the text. When I studied English literature, it became clear how easy it was to twist the text to support any opinion you want as opposed to examining what the author *actually said*. Explication and close readings were the least enjoyable assignments because they required you to *study the text*. That was far more difficult than it was to just write about your emotional response to what you thought the story meant. Parents and children must not back down from the challenge of studying the Bible as literature, especially when the content of the Bible undermines our cultural norms.

# Chapter 3: Matthew 18

The parables of Jesus are mentioned throughout a Christian's life. It is vital to understand them in the appropriate context since many are misinterpreted and taught in a way that is detrimental to children. Not even the disciples understood what Jesus was saying to them—he had to constantly repeat himself. With this in mind, it is not surprising that so many of the parables are misinterpreted today. Our children must be taught to stick to the text rigorously in order to develop their knowledge and the critical thinking skills necessary to understand what the parables mean. Using narration (or paraphrase) is a crucial tool in this effort.

## Lesson: Matthew 18:1-6

*"At that time the disciples came to Jesus, saying, 'Who is the greatest in the kingdom of heaven?' And calling to him a child, he put him in the midst of them, and said, 'Truly, I say to you, unless you turn and become like children, you will never enter the kingdom of heaven. Whoever humbles himself like this child, he is the greatest in the kingdom of heaven. Whoever receives one such child in my name receives me; but whoever causes one of these little ones who believe in me to sin, it would be better for him to have*

*a great millstone fastened round his neck and to be*
*drowned in the depth of the sea.'" (Matthew 18:1-6)*

- What did the disciples ask Jesus?

- What happens if somebody causes another
  person to sin?

- What is a millstone?

One of the great ironies of the Bible is that the disciples—
the people closest to Jesus—just can't seem to grasp the
message of the gospel. They're busy quibbling about who
is the greatest in the Kingdom of heaven instead of paying
attention to the things that Jesus is telling them. Jesus calls
a child to him in their midst and says, "become like
children". The common reaction is that Jesus is so
nice…he's telling the disciples to be childlike: "We should
be more like children—they're so humble and unselfish."
Any parent will tell you that kids are not humble and they
are quite possibly more self-centered than the disciples.
So, why is Jesus telling the disciples to become like
children? In the story's historical context, children are at
the bottom of the social hierarchy in the Roman
household. They are no better than slaves because they
are at the mercy of their father's authority until they come
of age. When Jesus says, "become like children," he is
commanding his disciples to become powerless and
totally dependent on God. This is a strange and difficult
concept to grasp in our modern society, where children

have authority over parents and, sadly, where the family's life revolves around the child, and not the parent.

## Discussion

Talk with children about what it was like to be a child in Jesus' time. Having this historical context in mind is critical for understanding the passage correctly. In ancient Rome, children were trained to obey those in authority without question. They were not allowed to talk back. If they did, they could get thrown out of the house and never allowed to return. Children had no rights. However, in St. Paul's biblical reworking of the Roman household, a father was no longer allowed to do or say whatever he wanted. St. Paul kept the Roman father's authority in place but transferred it from the individual person to the teaching of the Bible itself. The *paterfamilias* (the eldest male in the household) was now expected to speak and act according to Scripture when dealing with his family. The children were still expected to obey without question—not the *paterfamilias*—but the teaching of the Bible the *paterfamilias* was appointed to enforce. This point is reflected in Ephesians 6:1-4:

> *"Children obey your parents in the Lord, for this is right, 'Honor your father and mother' (this is the first commandment with a promise), 'that it may be well with you and that you may live long on the earth.' Fathers, do not provoke your children to anger, but bring them up in the discipline and instruction of the Lord.'"*

## Lesson: Matthew 18:7-9

*"Woe to the world for temptations to sin! For it is necessary that temptations come, but woe to the man by whom the temptation comes! And if your hand or your foot causes you to sin, cut it off and throw it away; it is better for you to enter life maimed or lame than with two hands or two feet to be thrown into the eternal fire. And if your eye causes you to sin, pluck it out and throw it away; it is better for you to enter life with one eye than with two eyes to be thrown into the hell of fire." (Matthew 18:7-9)*

- What does "temptation" mean?

- Does Jesus really mean to cut off your limbs if you sin?

Young kids might have some anxiety over this passage— does Jesus really want us to off our arms? You can assure them that this is not the case! What Jesus is (strongly) emphasizing is that the worst thing in the world we can do is cause another person to sin. Better that we commit the sin than have somebody else do it for us. One of the examples in the Bible would be the crucifixion itself. The Jews don't want the blood of Jesus on their hands so they deliver him to the Roman governor (Pilate) to do it for them. Those Gentiles are screwed anyways. Discuss with children (especially older teenagers) what this might look like in our modern times.

## *Discussion*

There are monastic orders that believe in self-flagellation. Look this term up if children do not know what it means. The dictionary defines it as "extreme criticism of one's self". This contradicts the Bible, since St. Paul explains that he will judge no one, not even himself (1 Corinthians 4:3), since only God is our Judge. Sadly, even Martin Luther practiced some form of self-flagellation. A group of people called the Flagellants roamed Europe in the 14th century and became particularly popular during the Black Plague. Talk with children about how this can be a form of self-righteousness. Despite the appearance of humility, self-flagellation actually turns the focus to one's own glory instead of God's judgment. Talk about how Jesus' warning emphasizes obedience to his teaching to avoid causing harm.

## Lesson: Matthew 18:10-14

*"See that you do not despise one of these little ones; for I tell you that in heaven their angels always behold the face of my Father who is in heaven. What do you think? If a man has a hundred sheep, and one of them has gone astray, does he not have the ninety-nine on the mountains and go in search of the one that went astray? And if he finds it, truly, I say to you, he rejoices over it more than over the ninety-nine that never went astray. So it is not the will of my Father*

*who is in heaven that one of these little ones should
perish." (Matthew 18:10-14)*

- Why are sheep used as an example in this
  passage?

Modern society has romanticized this image of Christ as
the shepherd going after one of his lost sheep. What they
fail to grasp is that this is actually an unflattering
comparison. In most descriptions of sheep, they are
observed to be unintelligent and of the herd mentality.
They are also susceptible to being prey—they do not
defend their territory and usually run away instead. If a
sheep gets lost, it's easy to envision a shepherd going after
it, muttering curses and irritation along the way. When it
is found, there is no joyous reunion...rather an
exasperated relief that the wayward animal has not done
itself in. This is a far cry from the romantic image of Jesus
tenderly cradling a lost sheep.

## Discussion

Children like sheep and may enjoy some historical facts
about them. Sheep were domesticated about 10,000 years
ago. Modern sheep are mostly descendants of the wild
Mouflon sheep in western Asia—though there may be
some others since domestication. While in the past sheep
were raised more for their wool, modern sheep
production is focused primarily on meat. If they are
raised for wool at all, it is for high quality fiber used for
knitting and weaving.

In *Storey's Guide to Raising Sheep,* there is an amusing poem called "The Shepherd's Lament". A few lines should sum up the perspective of the shepherd on sheep:

> *"Now I lay me down to sleep*
> *Exhausted by those doggone sheep...*
> *...I'm often asked why I raise sheep,*
> *With all the work*
> *and loss of sleep;*
> *...How can you explain,*
> *or even show?*
> *'Cause only a shepherd will ever know!"*

Ask children if they have ever seen sheep, whether at the zoo or on a farm. What would it be like to rescue a sheep? Look up Internet videos to see shepherds rescuing sheep. If possible, use videos from the Middle East, which provides the unique setting for shepherding in the Bible. It is quite amazing to see what shepherds will do to restore the sheep to their flock. Some children may ask why the shepherd doesn't just leave it there and buy a new one. Talk about how shepherds depend on sheep as their livelihood and how they don't always have the money to just go out and buy something new. This is also a good opportunity to discuss responsibility for things that one already owns.

## Lesson: Matthew 18:15-20

*"If your brother sins against you, go and tell him his fault, between you and him alone. If he listens to you,*

*you have gained your brother. But if he does not
listen, take one or two others along with you, that
every word may be confirmed by the evidence of two
or three witnesses. If he refuses to listen to them, tell
it to the church; and if he refuses to listen even to the
church, let him be to you as a Gentile and a tax
collector. Truly I say to you, whatever you bind on
earth shall be bound in heaven, and whatever you
loose on earth shall be loosed in heaven. Again I say
to you, if two of you agree on earth about anything
they ask, it will be done for them by my Father in
heaven. For where two or three are gathered in my
name, there am I in the midst of them." (Matthew
18:15-20)*

- What are you supposed to do if your
  brother sins against you?

- Is Jesus telling us to point out people's sins
  in this passage?

- Who is in the midst of where two or three
  are gathered?

People like to interpret this passage as a free license to
approach others to inform them of their sins. This has
become very apparent in churches that use it to gang up
on other church members (or non-members) whom they
perceive to be sinning. But consider it within the context
of the chapter. The overall point is to avoid causing your
fellow human being to sin, and that it is better for you to

sin than it is to cause someone else to stumble. The "you" here is a collective you—it is not individualistic. If someone is a direct threat to the community, then action must be taken. If direct confrontation doesn't work, then the person must bring a few others along "as witnesses". Not as accusers, but as *witnesses*. If the brother refuses to listen even after this, then involve the church. If it still doesn't work, wash hands of him and move on. It is imperative to remember that moving on from someone is not an indicator that you (collectively) are better than the offender. There should be no self-righteousness at all— the goal is to protect the community, not to put the offender down.

## *Discussion*

If you find yourself stuck for ideas on how to teach, take one word from the passage and have the children look it up. Remember, you do not have to have all the answers. You can learn alongside them. For example, the word "witness" has several different meanings: "attestation of fact or event," "one that gives evidence," or "something serving as evidence or proof". In the Bible, there are laws regarding witnesses. In Deuteronomy, two or three witnesses are required before putting someone to death (Deuteronomy 17:6). For any accusation in general, charges could only be sustained if two or three witnesses came forward with evidence (Deuteronomy 19:15). Leviticus tells us that if a witness knows something and does not come forward to speak, he shall "bear his

iniquity" (Leviticus 5:1). Talk with children about times
that they have had to be a witness in their own lives.

## Lesson: Matthew 18:21-35

*"Then Peter came up and said to him, 'Lord, how often
shall my brother sin against me, and I forgive him? As
many as seven times?' Jesus said to him, 'I do not say
to you seven times, but seventy times seven. Therefore
the kingdom of heaven maybe compared to a king who
wished to settle accounts with his servants. When he
began the reckoning, one was brought to him who
owed him ten thousand talents; and as he could not
pay, his lord ordered him to be sold, with his wife and
children and all that he had, and payment to be made.
So the servant fell on his knees, imploring him, 'Lord,
have patience with me, and I will pay you everything.'
And out of pity for him the lord of that servant
released him and forgave him the debt. But that same
servant, as he went out, came upon one of his fellow
servants who owed him a hundred denarii; and
seizing him by the throat he said, 'Pay what you owe.'
So his fellow servant fell down and besought him,
'Have patience with me, and I will pay you.' He
refused and went and put him in prison till he should
pay the debt. When his fellow servants saw what had
taken place, they were greatly distressed, and they
went and reported to their lord all that had taken
place. Then his lord summoned him and said to him,*

> 'You wicked servant! I forgave you all that debt
> because you besought me; and should not you have
> had mercy on your fellow servant, as I had mercy on
> you?' And in anger his lord delivered him to the
> jailers, till he should pay all his debt. So also my
> heavenly father will do to every one of you, if you do
> not forgive your brother from your heart.'" (Matthew
> 18:21-35)

- What is the importance of the numbers 7 and 70 in this passage?

- What is a "reckoning"?

- What are denarii?

- Why was the servant and his family going to be sold as slaves?

- Why did the lord forgive him?

- What did the servant do after he was released?

Kids may enjoy learning about the significance of different numbers. Seven is God's perfect number, so for Peter to ask Jesus if he should forgive his brother seven times, it is implied that this should be the right amount of forgiveness. However, the formula *seventy times seven* is made up of two perfect numbers: seven, which represents perfection; and seventy, which is made up of seven and ten. Ten is the number of completeness and God's law. The Romans counted in tens, suggesting that this completion is inclusive of the unclean gentiles. While the product of seven and seventy may not seem very high (490) in modern times, the point is to always forgive, even gentiles and the unclean.    God sets no limit on forgiveness.

## Discussion

Slavery is a topic that makes many people uncomfortable. Though slavery was common in ancient Roman society, it was often difficult to distinguish between a slave and a Roman citizen. Despite this, Roman masters had complete control over their slaves' lives. It was completely acceptable for a master to sell a slave (or his own children) if he was in need of money. Seneca, an ancient Roman poet and philosopher who was alive around the same time as Jesus, believed that slaves should be treated well because it would make them more productive. So, the king in this passage isn't necessarily a nice guy who is letting his slave off the hook. It's likely that the king decided that a happy, forgiven slave would bring him better fortune. If the slave knew a trade, he would be far more expensive to replace. Slaves that had skills were more costly than those without. Talk with children about forgiveness. Ask them how many times their parents expect them to forgive siblings.

# Chapter 4: Matthew 25

This passage is the answer to the lifelong question of "what should I do with my life"? This is a question that children—particularly teenagers—find themselves wondering. Even adults struggle with this as they search for meaning and purpose in their lives. The answer is that it doesn't matter what you do so long as you are productive and follow the teaching. Matthew 25 is not so much about the end times as much as it is a reminder to not waste the short time we have with pursuits that are irrelevant to the gospel. Do not allow cultural interpretation of "your special purpose" to influence this chapter. God is not interested in our individual talents so much as he is interested in what we do with our time here. Remember, this is not an "all about me and my world" curriculum. This is about God's world.

## Lesson: Matthew 25:1-13

*"Then the kingdom of heaven shall be compared to ten maidens who took their lamps and went to meet the bridegroom. Five of them were foolish, and five were wise. For when the foolish took their lamps, they took no oil with them; but the wise took flasks of oil with their lamps. As the bridegroom was delayed, they all slumbered and slept. But at midnight there was a cry,*

'Behold, the bridegroom! Come out to meet him.' Then all those maidens rose and trimmed their lamps. And the foolish said to the wise, 'Give us some of your oil, for our lamps are going out.' But the wise replied, 'Perhaps there will not be enough for us and for you; go rather to the dealers and buy for yourselves.' And while they went to buy, the bridegroom came, and those who were ready went in with him to the marriage feast; and the door was shut. Afterward, the other maidens came also, saying, 'Lord, lord, open to us.' But he replied, 'Truly, I say to you, I do not know you.' Watch therefore, for you know neither the day nor the hour." (Matthew 25:1-13)

- Why are the maidens waiting for the bridegroom?

- What does foolish mean?

- What does wise mean?

- What does the oil represent in this passage?

- Why didn't the wise maidens share their oil?

- What happened to the foolish maidens when they came back from buying oil?

## *Discussion*

As always, context is the key. Jesus is trying to explain something to the disciples who have asked about the close of the age. Consider, then, what the oil represents in this passage. The oil is the teaching—you have either studied it or you have not. Children may wonder why the wise maidens didn't share their oil. When you study for a test, you have the information, as opposed to a friend who didn't study. When it comes time to take the test, you cannot share what you have learned. You can only do your best and pray for mercy.

Talk with children about the wedding. This is also a good opportunity to learn about traditions in different cultures. In Palestinian wedding traditions, the bridegroom comes to fetch the bride. This is an age-old custom that is still practiced in modern Palestine—not simply to preserve tradition, but to do so as an act of rebellion against the suppression of their culture.

 Wedding preparation can last for several days before the actual ceremony. The bridegroom is shaven and cleaned up before presenting himself to the bride. The bride is adorned with henna on the day of the ceremony and, upon the arrival of the bridegroom, declares herself a "good girl" who has not dishonored her family. Then everyone goes to the wedding feast. It is a way for the family to come together and connect, especially for those who live further away. For Palestinians, there is nothing more important than the family unit. With this in mind, let us examine the behavior of the foolish maidens.

If students are not familiar with the term "foolish", have them look it up. Foolish in Greek is *moros,* which means "dull" or "stupid". The foolish maidens were stupid enough to not plan ahead and bring oil with them. *Phronimos* is the Greek word for "wise"—also meaning "intelligent, sensible, and prudent". The wise maidens planned ahead and brought enough oil to last until the arrival of the bridegroom.

Children might wonder why the wise maidens tell the foolish to go and get their own oil instead of sharing what they brought. But sharing is not the point of the passage— the point is that the oil represents the teaching and five of them received it and five of them didn't. Jesus is trying to explain that you either prepared yourself for the last day by studying Torah or by wasting your time. And since you don't know when exactly the bridegroom is coming, you'd better be ready. Compare it to studying for a pop quiz—you don't know when the teacher is going to give it to you, but you had better be prepared. Stress the importance of studying the Bible to prepare for life.

## Lesson: Matthew 25:14-30

*"For it will be as when a man going on a journey called his servants and entrusted to them his property; to one he gave five talents, to another two,*

to another one, to each according to his ability. Then
he went away. He who had received the five talents
went at once and traded with them; and he made five
talents more. So also, he who had the two talents
made two talents more. But he who had received the
one talent went and dug in the ground and hid his
master's money. Now after a long time the master of
those servants came and settled accounts with them.
And he who had received the five talents came
forward, bringing five talents more, saying, 'Master,
you delivered to me five talents; here I have made five
more.' His master said to him, 'Well done, good and
faithful servant; you have been faithful over a little, I
will set you over much; enter into the joy of your
master.' And he also who had the two talents; here I
have made two talents more.' His master said to him,
'Well done, good and faithful servant; you have been
faithful over a little, I will set you over much; enter
into the joy of your master.' He also who had received
the one talent came forward, saying, 'Master, I knew
you to be a hard man, reaping where you did not sow,
and gathering where you did not winnow; so I was
afraid, and I went and hid your talent in the ground.
Here you have what is yours.' But his master
answered him, 'You wicked and slothful servant! You
knew that I reap where I have not sowed, and gather
where I have not winnowed? Then you ought to have
invested my money with the bankers, and at my
coming I should have received what was my own with
interest. So take the talent from him and give it to him

*who has the ten talents. For to everyone who has more will be given, and he will have abundance; but from him who has not, even what he has will be taken away. And cast the worthless servant into the outer darkness; there men will weep and gnash their teeth."'* (Matthew 25:14-30)

- What is a talent?

- What does "servant" mean?

- What happened to the two servants who did something with their talent?

- What happened to the servant who did nothing?

## Discussion

Ask children what they think "talent" means. It is not uncommon for people to associate "talent" with our modern definition of the word. This passage is often used to encourage people to develop their "gifts" in order to live out their unique purpose or as a guide to investing material wealth. Do not fall into this trap. This is not an allegory about our unique flair or stock portfolios. The talents described here are units of measurement. A talent typically consisted of 3000 shekels—the weight varied depending on whether or not the talent was made up of silver or gold. But the talent is not a metaphor for our special gifts. Consider the context of the chapter, which is about preparing for the arrival of God. God is not interested in our unique flair, he is interested in whether or not we did anything useful with the teaching before the judgment. The talent is a metaphor for the Torah. We have the gospel now…what are we going to do with it? What does it mean to use the teaching in our lives? It doesn't matter if the talent is large or small. We have no excuse once we have been given charge of it. Discuss with children what that might look like for them. What does living out the gospel look like on a day to day basis? What happens if we do nothing?

The term "servant" here is an important concept to discuss with children. The Greek word for servant is *"doulos"* and the Hebrew word is *"ebed"*. But it doesn't actually mean "servant"—it means "slave". The term is used almost exclusively throughout the Bible and yet you never see it translated as "slave"…it's always "servant". Slavery has such stigma attached to it that Calvin and John Knox and other translators of the sixteenth century decided to soften the blow with "servant". But words matter. Servant implies that you have better standing. Servant makes us think of Downton Abbey. But the word is actually "slave". We are meant to be slaves. The servants here are not servants…they are slaves. They were not employed by their master—they are owned. They are at the mercy of their master—as we are at the mercy of our Master.

## Lesson: Matthew 25:31-46

*"When the Son of man comes in his glory, and all the angels with him, then he will sit on his glorious throne. Before him will be gathered all the nations and he will separate them one from another as a shepherd separates the sheep from the goats, and he will place the sheep at his right hand, but the goats at the left. Then the King will say to those at his right hand, 'Come, O blessed of my Father, inherit the kingdom prepared for you from the foundation of the world; for I was hungry and you gave me food, I was thirsty and you gave me drink, I was a stranger and you welcomed me, I was naked and you clothed me, I was sick and you visited me, I was in prison and you came to me.' Then the righteous will answer him, 'Lord, when did we see thee hungry and feed thee, or thirsty and give thee drink? And when did we see thee a stranger and welcome thee, or naked and clothe thee? And when did we see thee sick or in prison and visit thee?' And the King will answer them, 'Truly, I say to you, as you did it to one of the least of these my brethren, you did it to me.' "Then he will say to those at his left hand, 'Depart from me, you cursed, into the eternal fire prepared for the devil and his angels; for I was hungry and you gave me no food, I was thirsty and you gave me no drink, I was a stranger and you did not welcome me, naked and you did not clothe me, sick and in prison and you did not visit me.' Then they also will answer, 'Lord, when did*

*we see thee hungry or thirsty or a stranger or naked or*
*sick or in prison, and did not minister to thee?' Then*
*he will answer them, 'Truly, I say to you, as you did*
*it not to one of the least of these, you did it not to me.'*
*And they will go away into eternal punishment, but*
*the righteous into eternal life." (Matthew 25: 31-46)*

- What do sheep and goats represent in this
  passage?

- What does the Lord say the righteous did?

- What does he say that the unrighteous did?

## Discussion

Sheep are often used in the Bible to represent the people.
The fact that sheep are stupid and stubborn makes sense
when applied to us; but when the metaphor is applied to
Jesus, it makes less sense. When sheep are properly
trained, they are obedient. They will follow their master
wherever he goes. Hartley's "Researches in Greece and
the Levant" remarks upon the "prompt obedience" of a
well-trained sheep when the shepherd calls it by name.
Jesus obeys, like a sheep, unto his death. We are called to
the same level of obedience. Children will understand all
about obedience. Adults may reject this idea or feel
uncomfortable with the idea of "prompt obedience"
because of past experiences with spiritual abusers who
demanded unquestioning compliance or because their
ego simply resists the notion. The idea of training our
children to be obedient to authority (other than our own)

may not rest well. Recall the soldier from the earlier chapter—the centurion who was obedient and trusted in Jesus' authority. I often worry about training my own children to be obedient to authority because one day they may run into someone who abuses them. But then I remember that I am training them to obey a wise teaching that will help them navigate abuse in the world. I know also that I must be obedient to this teaching and trust God to care for my children, even through suffering. This doesn't mean not taking steps to protect my children— but it is a good reminder in this day of helicopter parenting that I can't control every moment of their lives.

Talk with children about wasted time. This passage presents an example of time not wasted. We are shown that those who were productive fed the hungry, clothed the needy, cared for the sick, and had compassion for criminals. But lest we feel self-righteous about it, remember, sheep are still stupid, stubborn animals. Google "sheep sorting" and watch the videos of the process farmers go through to sort their sheep. Kids and adults alike will enjoy watching the sheep bottleneck and try to climb over each other as the farmers try to direct them where they want them to go. It is tedious, difficult, and hilarious. Sheep are not smart. It completely changes your image of the last judgment where sheep and goats are sorted. This is not a flattering metaphor.

Discuss with children what our time on earth should look like. What pursuits align with the gospel message? What doesn't match up with what God expects from us?

In Matthew 25 Jesus is warning us not to worry so much about what's going to happen at the end—we will all be judged—but to focus our energy on ensuring that we do not waste the time and teaching (or talent) that we have been given. A life devoted to obedience, work, service, and study is a life well lived. When the Master returns, let us be able to say, "Look, Master, here are ten talents!" instead of telling him we hid our piece in a hole in the ground.

# Chapter 5: The Pauline Epistles

People struggle with teaching St. Paul's epistles to children. Perhaps they simply skip it altogether. This stems from the wrong assumption that they need to have fully mastered the epistles in order to explain them to others. I've often heard parents and educators comment, "I don't know enough to teach this to children. I don't understand it, how can I teach it to anyone else?" One does not need to have spent years in seminary to be able to read the Bible and to teach it to others. Once again, a parent or educator need only be willing to learn alongside children, to admit when they don't have the answer, and to admit their mistakes when the text contradicts something they believe or may have previously taught. Learning together is important—an act of obedience—especially with older children.

## 1 Corinthians 13

Modern culture demands that our children grow up faster than ever before and presents them with challenges even parents struggle to handle. We want our kids to grow up looking at the world through a Scriptural lens. When it comes to community and family, our children (and we ourselves!) must think scripturally in a world that preaches a misguided understanding of love.

While the following sections are intended for teaching teenagers, they are also helpful for younger students. Let's begin by examining 1 Corinthians 13 to get to a better understanding of what biblical love entails.

As always, it is better to understand this chapter within the context of the entire book. 1 Corinthians is a letter to the Corinthian church regarding their arrogance and cruel behavior towards the weak and unbelievers. This is a terrific epistle for modern Christians. Self-righteousness remains a major problem in modern religious communities. Paul's strong words to the Corinthians still ring true today.

## Lesson: 1 Corinthians 13:1-3

*"If I speak in the tongues of men and angels, but have not love, I am a noisy gong or a clanging cymbal. And if I have prophetic powers, and understand all mysteries and all knowledge, and if I have all faith, so as to remove mountains, but have not love, I am nothing. If I give away all I have, and if I deliver my body to be burned, but have not love, I gain nothing."* (1 Corinthians 13:1-3)

Have older students summarize the passage. If necessary, prompt them with the following questions:

- Looking at the broader context of the passage, what is St. Paul's definition of "love?"

- What does it mean to "speak in tongues"?

- What is Paul emphasizing in this passage?

## *Discussion*

In a chapter about love, it is essential to have a correct understanding of the term. In Hebrew, the word for love, *ahava,* is made up of three different letters. The letters are then broken down into two parts: "I give" and "I love". The Greek word for love, *agape,* is also communal, in the sense that one has affection and goodwill towards others in the community. Merriam-Webster defines love as "strong affection arising out of personal ties" (e.g. maternal love for a child) and "attraction based on sexual desire". Clearly our definition of love has undergone some changes over time. Today, love is less about giving and more about how others relate to us or make us feel. Modern notions of love are inward looking and selfish, with little or no regard for others or the needs of the community at large. Talk with children about what love means in modern English compared with the Hebrew and the Greek words.

Older (and younger) children may be curious about what is meant by "tongues". If they have a Protestant, Pentecostal, or non-denominational background, they may have experienced adults speaking in tongues during a church service. This will sound like complete gibberish to the listeners. It is interesting to note that "tongues" here are defined by some as any language that the community does not understand. So, it may not be a mystical language bestowed by God. Instead, it could be the ability to speak other languages outside of the community's mother tongue. Paul does not care either way. He attacks the Corinthians for their arrogance. There is no value in speaking in tongues if it does not benefit the community. If the community doesn't understand you, you are simply showing off. Note that when the apostles spoke in tongues in Acts, everyone in the room could understand them.

## Lesson: 1 Corinthians 13:4-7

*"Love is patient and kind; love is not jealous or boastful; it is not arrogant or rude. Love does not insist on its own way; it is not irritable or resentful; it does not rejoice at wrong, but rejoices in the right. Love bears all things, believes all things, hopes all things, endures all things." (1 Corinthians 13: 4-7)*

Have older students summarize the passage. If necessary, prompt them with the following questions:

- How is love defined in this passage?

- What does it mean to bear all things?

- Can you give examples of times when you were not loving according to St. Paul's teaching?

## Discussion

A troubling line in this passage is one that is frequently used to rationalize judgment of others "[Love] does not rejoice at wrong but rejoices in the right". It is here that the Bible is used as a telescope rather than a magnifying glass: we use it to look at what others are doing instead of turning it inward to view our own sins. Love in 1 Corinthians 13 is not a checklist for the noble Christians to feel kindly towards their heathen brethren. It is not support for Christians to publicly denounce their neighbor in the name of "love". It is a reminder to Christians that even if you follow all the rules—even if you do everything that you are supposed to do—if you do not love your neighbor, it means nothing.

Modern Christians love to point out how wrong everyone else is. We spend so much time focusing on what we see as the sins of others that we overlook what we need to fix in ourselves. We arrogantly judge Muslims, immigrants, refugees, and homosexuals. Our behavior is that of a colonizing country: everyone in the world needs to be exactly like us, and only then can we understand the world. Everyone else needs to change, except us. We have the right way. We know how it's done. We conceitedly cry out in the name of love that everyone else is wrong. As Deacon Henok of the Tewahido Bible Study podcast once said, "The Bible is meant to be used as a magnifying glass for ourselves; not a telescope to examine what others are doing." We need to stop using Scripture as a tool for measuring others and use it to measure ourselves.

Our modern world teaches us to place our own needs over the needs of others. We are told not to submit to our spouse, but to follow our heart. In many cases we follow our heart to someone else, only to discover that we must submit to them too. So we run to another, and the cycle of infidelity continues. Modern love is portrayed as a feeling or emotional high that we must constantly chase, rather than the product of hard work and steadfast commitment. Discuss with teens what some examples of love within marriage might look like.

## Lesson: 1 Corinthians 13:8-13

*"Love never ends; as for prophecies, they will pass away; as for tongues, they will cease; as for knowledge, it will pass away. For our knowledge is imperfect and our prophecy is imperfect; but when the perfect comes, the imperfect will pass away. When I was a child, I spoke like a child, I reasoned like a child; when I became a man, I gave up childish ways. For now we see in a mirror dimly, but then face to face. Now I know in part; then I shall understand fully, even as I have been fully understood. So faith, hope, love abide, these three; but the greatest of these is love." (1 Corinthians 13:8-13)*

Have students summarize the passage. If necessary, prompt them with the following question:

- Why is love emphasized over knowledge?

- How is St. Paul's use of the word "child" here different that Jesus' use in Matthew?

## *Discussion*

This passage is reminiscent of Ecclesiastes. While everything else passes away, love remains. Everything but love is impermanent, as the Buddhists say. Tongues don't matter; knowledge does not matter. The only thing that matters is whether we love our neighbor. On the day of judgment, we will see God face-to-face and will have to answer for the life we chose to live. Did we place value on love or did we live arrogantly for things that do not matter? Talk with students about what it means to behave like a child. Children are selfish. A true adult understands that he must make sacrifices for others. Modern Western culture is full of adult children who live for themselves and do whatever pleases them, under the pretext of "following their heart," but it is childish to do whatever you want to do. An adult sees what must to be done for the sake of others and does it, even at the expense of their own comfort.

## Galatians 4

The gospel stories can seem simpler to teach to children because most of the parables are action oriented. Jesus is always going somewhere and doing something interesting, which makes it easy to follow the narrative. The Epistles are more challenging because the concepts are more abstract. Even adults struggle with Paul's letters and the idea of teaching it to children is daunting. Children may also struggle because they don't understand. The role of the educator is to foster familiarity with the written words of the Epistles and to help children understand these words by using examples from everyday life—situations with family, at school, and even at church. Remember, you don't have to provide all the answers. You need only present the Bible to your students and let God do the rest.

Galatians 4 is the chapter appointed for the Feast of the Nativity. The lectionary selection is limited to verses 4-7, but for the sake of context, it is essential to study the whole chapter. Paul wrote to the Galatians about whether it was necessary for a Gentile to become a Jew before becoming a Christian. Paul was against this idea. We can help children understand this concept by taking these passages and explaining them with examples from everyday life. Should people be forced to become "like us" in order to follow Jesus?

## Lesson: Galatians 4:1-7

*"I mean that the heir, as long as he is a child, is no better than a slave, though he is owner of all the estate; but he is under guardians and trustees until the date set by the father. So with us; when we were children, we were slaves to the elemental spirits of the universe. But when the time had fully come, God sent forth his Son, born of woman, born under the law, to redeem those who were under the law, so that we might receive adoption as sons. And because you are sons, God has sent the Spirit of his Son into our hearts, crying, 'Abba! Father!' So through God you are no longer a slave but a son, and if a son then an heir."* (Galatians 4:1-7)

> Have students summarize the passage. If necessary, prompt them with the following questions:
>
> - Who is the woman that God's Son was born to?
>
> - What does Paul mean when he says that a child is no better than a slave?

## Discussion

In ancient Roman society, you could not tell children and slaves apart. A Roman father could choose who he wanted to be his son and beneficiary of his inheritance. This meant that he could choose a slave if he wanted to and could make a slave his son! Paul is telling the Galatians that God can choose whoever he wants to be his son or daughter. God is the father of all, not just the Jews, or in our context, the Christians.

- What does it mean if God is the father of all?

- How does this shape how we view others?

If God is the father of all, then everyone is our family. If we say "family first", according to the Bible that means that *everyone* is first.  *Everyone* is a child of God, and therefore, we should treat *everyone* as if they are family. Jesus said "love your neighbor". Talk about how the children are expected to treat family members and how they could incorporate this into their lives at school or even church.

## Lesson: Galatians 4:8-20

*"Formerly, when you did not know God, you were in bondage to beings that by nature are no gods; but now that you have come to know God, or rather to be known by God, how can you turn back again to the weak and beggarly elemental spirits, whose slaves you want to be once more? You observe days, and months, and seasons, and years! I am afraid I have labored over you in vain. Brethren, I beseech you, become as I am, for I also have become as you are. You did me no wrong; you know it was because of a bodily*

*ailment that I preached the gospel to you at first; and though my condition was a trial to you, you did not scorn or despise me, but received me as an angel of God, as Christ Jesus. What has become of the satisfaction you felt? For I bear you witness that, if possible, you would have plucked out your eyes and given them to me. Have I then become your enemy by telling you the truth? They make much of you, but for no good purpose; they want to shut you out, that you may make much of them. For good purpose it is always good to be made much of, and not only when I am present with you. My little children, with whom I am again in travail until Christ be formed in you! I could wish to be present with you now and to change my tone, for I am perplexed about you." (Galatians 4:8-20)*

Have students summarize the passage. If necessary, prompt them with the following questions:

- What are "elemental spirits"?

- Why does Paul feel he has labored over the Galatians in vain?

- What does he mean when he says "become as I am"?

- What bodily ailment is Paul talking about?

## Discussion

Students may want to know what Paul means by "elemental spirits". The Greek word *stoicheia* is often translated as "principles of the world". This can mean anything outside of the teaching to which Paul assigns authority for the Galatians. It could refer to paganism or to smooth talking opponents of Paul's teaching. Now that the Galatians have been freed by knowing the true God, Paul doesn't understand why they would want to go back to being slaves to a false teaching. Recall in Exodus how the Israelites cried for a return to slavery in Egypt because they were hungry:

> *"And the whole congregation of the people of Israel murmured against Moses and Aaron in the wilderness, and said to them, "Would that we had died by the hand of the Lord in the land of Egypt, when we sat by the fleshpots and ate bread to the full; for you have brought us out into this wilderness to kill this whole assembly with hunger."*
> *(Exodus 16:2-3)*

Although the Galatians were initially receptive to Paul's message and cared for him while he was ill, they were easily wooed back into bondage by proponents of false principles. Paul is disappointed. Although these advocates "make much" of them, they are doing it for their own purposes. In modern times, people like to talk about how good they are, especially Christians. They forget that "no one is good but God", and flock instead to pastors who pat them on the back and tell them it's all going to be fine and that they're "good" people. The problem is "out there" with those "other" people—the ones who don't look and act like us. The Galatians have fallen into the trap of flattery. Talk with teens about being influenced by principles of the world at school or in church. The fact that these things occur at church can make it tricky because we assume that if we heard it in the sermon, it must be true and it must be Scriptural. This is incorrect and a lazy way of thinking. This is why children must learn to read the text and think for themselves so that they can recognize false principles dressed up as "Christianity". What things might we ascribe authority to that do not coincide with the written teaching?

## Lesson: Galatians 4:21-31

*"Tell me, you who desire to be under law, do you not hear the law? For it is written that Abraham had two sons, one by a slave and one by a free woman. But the son of the slave was born according to the flesh, the son of the free woman through promise. Now this is an allegory: these women are two covenants. One is from Mount Sinai, bearing children for slavery; she is Hagar. Now Hagar is Mount Sinai in Arabia; she corresponds to the present Jerusalem, for she is in slavery with her children. But the Jerusalem above is free, and she is our mother. For it is written, 'Rejoice, O barren one who does not bear; break forth and shout, you who are in travail; for the children of the*

*desolate one are many more than the children of her*
*that is married.' Now we, brethren, like Isaac, are*
*children of promise. But as at that time he who was*
*born according to the flesh persecuted him who was*
*born according to the Spirit, so it is now. But what*
*does the scripture say? 'Cast out the slave and her*
*son; for the son of the slave shall not inherit with the*
*son of the free woman' So, brethren, we are not*
*children of the slave but of the free woman."*
*(Galatians 4:21-31)*

Have students summarize the passage. If
necessary, prompt them with the following
questions:

- What is the name of the slave in this
  passage?

- Who is the free woman?

- Who are the two sons of Abraham?

- What is an allegory?

- Where is Mount Sinai?

## Discussion

Paul directs their minds to the law, since they want to be
under it. What does the law really say? It says that
Abraham had two sons, "one by a slave and one by a free
woman". The son of the slave was born "according to the

flesh", or rather, Abraham and Sarah's attempt to control their seed. If the students are not familiar with the story the passage is referring to, stop and go back to Genesis (Genesis 16; Genesis 17: 1-21).

An allegory is a story that has a moral or political meaning. It is used in literature to give depth to the author's work. Allegory stems from the Latin word *allegoria*, which is a "description of one thing under the image of another". The Bible is full of allegories, but it is not always easy to spot them. Here the allegory refers to two biblical characters: the first, who follows all the rules and, the second, who is abusive. In the in the story of Hagar and Sarah, Hagar does everything that she is supposed to do and gets kicked out. Sarah abuses Hagar and becomes the mother of nations. This apparent injustice is meant to illustrate that God can do whatever he wants with whomever he wants. He can turn even an abuser into an instrument of his purpose. People often interpret this passage as "isn't that great, we're children of the free woman". But Sarah was not a very likable character. She was manipulative, vindictive, and had no qualms about throwing Hagar and her child out into the desert to die. Hurrah, we're children of the free woman.

Mount Sinai is in Egypt. It is significant in both Christian and Islamic traditions. For Christians, it is where Moses spoke to God and received the Ten Commandments. There is currently an Orthodox monastery (St. Catherine's) built at the foot of the mountain in 530 AD)—

the oldest continuously inhabited monastery in the world.

# Chapter 6: Matthew 26-28

The final section of my book is the most lengthy, because it deals with Matthew's passion narrative, which may be the most important story in the Bible. Christians tend to gloss over the Crucifixion and focus solely on the Resurrection. In a misplaced effort to focus on the positive, we forget that without the Crucifixion there is no Resurrection. It is in the Crucifixion that we find the ultimate portrayal of Jesus' obedience and are reminded of our duty to perform the same obedience, even unto death. While the final two chapters of this book are intended for a teenage audience, it is possible to discuss this story with young children as well. Younger students may even have a better understanding than teenagers since they have no choice but to offer the same *unquestioning obedience*—a kind of blind trust in the wisdom of their parents. However, teens are more capable of grasping abstract concepts and putting them into their own words. Again, narration is a very useful tool when teaching teenagers and is a valuable skill that will assist them in their lifelong study of the Bible.

## Lesson: Matthew 26:1-16

*"When Jesus had finished all these sayings, he said to his disciples, 'You know that after two days the*

89

Passover is coming, and the Son of man will be
delivered up to be crucified.'

"Then the chief priests and the elders of the people
gathered in the palace of the high priest, who was
called Ca'iaphas, and took counsel together in order
to arrest Jesus by stealth and kill him. But they said,
'Not during the feast, lest there be a tumult among the
people.'

"Now when Jesus was at Bethany in the house of
Simon the leper, a woman came up to him with an
alabaster flask of very expensive ointment, and she
poured it on his head, as he sat at table. But when the
disciples saw it, they were indignant, saying, 'Why
this waste? For this ointment might have been sold
for a large sum, and given to the poor.' But Jesus,
aware of this, said to them, 'Why do you trouble the
woman? For she has done a beautiful thing to me. For
you always have the poor with you, but you will not
always have me. In pouring this ointment on my body
she has done it to prepare me for burial. Truly, I say
to you, wherever this gospel is preached in the whole
world, what she has done will be told in memory of
her.'

"Then one of the twelve, who was called Judas
Iscariot, went to the chief priests and said, 'What will
you give me if I deliver him to you?' And they paid
him thirty pieces of silver. And from that moment he

*sought an opportunity to betray him." (Matthew 26: 1-16)*

Have the teens paraphrase what the passage is about. You can help prompt them with the following questions if they are having difficulties. They shouldn't require as much prompting as younger children, who may not yet be able to summarize what they've heard.

**What is the Passover?**

- Why don't the chief priests and elders want to arrest Jesus during the feast?

- Jesus is hanging out at Simon the leper's house. Why is this a big deal?

- Why are the disciples upset over the woman's gift to Jesus?

- What does Jesus say to them?

- How much does Judas get for betraying Jesus? Is the number thirty significant? Why?

## Discussion

There may be some confusion over what the Passover feast is, particularly if children are not familiar with the Old Testament. Refer to the Exodus story and how God slew the firstborn of Egypt while "passing over" the children of the Hebrews. (Exodus 12) In this story, the

Hebrew people are commanded to sacrifice a lamb on the tenth day of the first month of the year. They were to take blood and smear it on the door so that the Lord would know to pass over the house.

It is worth pointing out to students that while the chief priests and elders are very conscious of following religious rules (for example, not arresting Jesus during the Passover for fear of inciting mob wrath), they seem to have little regard for the meaning of those rules and which rules take priority. Teens are big on pointing out hypocrisy. Throughout his ministry, Jesus continually refers the Pharisees back to the Torah, for example, when the Scribe questions Jesus (Mark 12:28-34). In the text in Mark, the Scribe is looking to see if Jesus' teaching aligns with the Torah. Jesus answers correctly (Deuteronomy 6:4-5) and the Scribe is satisfied. People want to dismiss the Old Testament because of an incorrect assumption that Jesus is here to replace it with the New Testament, making it irrelevant. Therefore, they argue, an understanding of the Torah is not necessary. But reading the New Testament without a thorough understanding of the Old Testament is futile and deeply problematic. When people say that Jesus came to break the rules of the old Law, they are wrong. Jesus is actually reinforcing and preaching the Torah—correcting misunderstandings and redirecting the peoples' focus back to God. The problem the Pharisees have with Jesus is that he is calling out their lack of understanding and exposing their desire to promote themselves in God's name while putting others down. Talk with students about examples in the modern world. Have they seen this problem at school, in politics, or in church? Have they found themselves or seen others acting like the Pharisees?

The misunderstanding of Torah is exemplified in the passage about the woman who anoints Jesus with expensive oil while he is having dinner with Simon the leper. The disciples, who are very likely already uncomfortable because they are in the house of a sick, social outcast, complain that money has been wasted: "For this ointment ought to have been sold for a large sum and given to the poor." Instead of considering the possibility that this woman may have spent what little she had on the perfume to honor Jesus, the disciples criticize her for not using it for what they deem more practical purposes. You can liken this to complaints about money typical of church committees. The poor, Jesus reminds the disciples, you will always have with you, but you will not always have me. Why do we always have the needy with us? Because they are the right hand of the Lord and a judgment against us. The impoverished are set before us in the same way that Jesus was publicly shamed—to remind us that we are failing because we ignore the cry of those who are hungry, even as we live in comfort. In St. Paul's letters, "the poor" are also a euphemism for those who have not yet heard the gospel, or worse, who have heard but don't understand and are unable to teach correctly. On every level, in Scripture, the poor are a painful and inconvenient truth. Talk with students about this truth. What does it mean to have people living in poverty in a country as wealthy as ours?

## Lesson: Matthew 26:20-25

*"Now on the first day of Unleavened Bread the disciples came to Jesus, saying, 'Where will you have us prepare for you to eat the Passover?' He said, "Go into the city to a certain one, and say to him, 'The Teacher says, My time is at hand; I will keep the Passover at your house with my disciples.' And the disciples did as Jesus had directed them, and they prepared the Passover.*

*"When it was evening, he sat at table with the twelve disciples; and as they were eating, he said, 'Truly, I say to you, one of you will betray me.' And they were truly sorrowful, and began to say to him one after another, 'Is it I, Lord?' He answered, 'He who has dipped his hand in the dish with me, will betray me. The Son of man goes as it is written of him, but woe to that man by whom the Son of man is betrayed! It would have been better for that man if he had not been born.' Judas, who betrayed him, said, 'Is it I, Master?' He said to him, 'You have said so.'" (Matthew 26:20-25)*

Ask the students to put the passage into their own words. Use the following questions to prompt them if they are having difficulty.

- What did Jesus tell his disciples while they were sitting at table together?

- What did the disciples say in response?

- Jesus tells them that "he who has dipped his hand in the dish with me, will betray me." To whom is Jesus referring?

## Discussion

Ask students who Jesus is talking about when he says someone will betray him. It is easy to assume that this passage is referring to Judas, since he is the most obvious betrayer. However, Jesus is being intentionally ambiguous when he says "he who has dipped his hand in the dish with me"—he's not specifically calling out Judas—he could be calling out any one of the disciples. *All of them* are going to betray him in one way or another, as we will see in later passages. Note that all the disciples, including Judas, ask the same question, "Is it I?" When Judas asks the question, Jesus answers, "You have said so." But considering the entire story, the question, "Is it I," left unanswered, is equally uncomfortable. No one is excused, including the reader. One betrayal is not worse than another. All fall short and all are equally under judgment.

## Lesson: Matthew 26:26-35

*"Now as they were eating, Jesus took bread, and blessed, and broke it, and gave it to the disciples and said, 'Take, eat; this is my body." And he took a cup, and when he had given thanks he gave it to them, saying, 'Drink of it, all of you; for this is my blood of the covenant, which is poured out for many for the forgiveness of sins. I tell you I shall not drink again of this fruit of the vine until that day when I drink it new with you in my Father's kingdom.'*

*"And when they had sung a hymn, they went out to the Mount of Olives. Then Jesus said to them, 'You will all fall away because of me this night; for it is written, "I will strike the shepherd, and the sheep of the flock will be scattered." But after I am raised up, I will go before you to Galilee.' Peter declared to him, 'Though they all fall away because of you, I will never fall away.' Jesus said to him, 'Truly, I say to you, this very night, before the cock crows, you will deny me three times.' Peter said to him, 'Even if I must die with you, I will not deny you.' And so said all the disciples." (Matthew 26:26-35)*

Have the students summarize the passage in their own words. If they have trouble, prompt them with the following questions:

- What does Jesus mean when he says he will not "drink again of this fruit of the vine until that day when I drink it new with you in my Father's kingdom"?

- Peter continues to insist that he is the only loyal disciple of Jesus. What is Jesus' response?

## Discussion

In addition to narration, ask the students to relate what they are reading to their own lives. Is there anything familiar about this passage (or any of the passages) that can be compared to examples in everyday life?

Peter likes to be the center of attention. Throughout the gospel, he is always popping up and insisting upon his worthiness. Yet he is easily shaken, as demonstrated when he walked out on the water to Jesus and sank (Matthew 14: 22-33). Peter is that guy who is always running his mouth. We all know that guy. We should not be surprised, then, when he swears that he will never, ever, ever betray Jesus, even if everyone else does. But Jesus knows better and calls him out on it. We all like to think that we would be capable of loyalty in the darkest hour but it's clear here that even those who were closest to Jesus were incapable. If those who spent their days with him in person were unable to stand fast beside Jesus during his loneliest period, what chance have we in our current day and age?

### Lesson: Matthew 26:47-56

*"Then Jesus went with them to a place called Gethsem'ane, and he said to his disciples, 'Sit here, while I go yonder and pray.' And taking with him Peter and the two sons of Zeb'edee, he began to be sorrowful and troubled. Then he said to them, 'My*

*soul is very sorrowful, even to death; remain here, and watch with me.' And going a little farther he fell on his face and prayed, 'My Father, if it be possible, let this cup pass from me; nevertheless, not as I will, but as thou wilt.' And he came to the disciples and found them sleeping; and he said to Peter, 'So, could you not watch with me one hour? Watch and pray that you may not enter into temptation; the spirit indeed is willing, but the flesh is weak.' Again, for the second time, he went away and prayed, 'My Father, if this cannot pass unless I drink it, thy will be done.' And again he came and found them sleeping, for their eyes were heavy. So, leaving them again, he went away and prayed for the third time, saying the same words. Then he came to the disciples and said to them, 'Are you still sleeping and taking your rest? Behold, the hour is at hand, and the Son of man is betrayed into the hands of sinners. Rise, let us be going; see, my betrayer is at hand.'" (Matthew 26:36-46)*

Have the students paraphrase the passage. If they have trouble, prompt them with the following questions:

- Where did Jesus and the disciples go?

- What did he ask them to do when they arrived?

- Who did he take with him?

- What did he ask Peter and the sons of Zeb'edee to do?

- What did he pray for when he was alone?

- Were his disciples able to stay awake?

- How many times did Jesus ask God to remove the cup from him?

## Discussion

Jesus goes away from the house where he and the disciples celebrate the Passover. Then he takes a few disciples with him and asks them to keep watch while he prays. They are clueless—Jesus is under duress and terrified. But they don't notice. Jesus knows what's coming and he asks God for a way out. But in the end, he submits to God's will. There is that word again, *submit*. The word that we modern folk hate so much. It is difficult to comprehend submitting to God when he asks us to die for him.

Talk with students about what it means to submit. What examples can they take from their everyday lives? Have they ever been afraid to follow the directions of their parents or elders because it meant they would have to suffer embarrassment?

Here Peter is given a test and fails miserably. It calls to mind Luke 16:10:

*"He who is faithful in a very little is faithful also in much; and he who is dishonest in a very little is dishonest also in much. If then you have not been faithful in the*

*unrighteous mammon, who will entrust to you the true riches? And if you have not been faithful in that which is another's, who will give you that which is your own? No servant can serve two masters; for either he will hate the one and love the other, or he will be devoted to the one and despise the other. You cannot serve God and mammon."*

Peter cannot even keep watch without falling asleep. If he can't be faithful in this small thing, how will he be loyal to Jesus in the events to follow and beyond? He doesn't. He fails. It's a foreshadowing of Peter's betrayal yet to come. And it's not just Peter, it's all the disciples.

## Lesson: Matthew 26:47-56

*'While he was still speaking, Judas came, one of the twelve, and with him a great crowd with swords and clubs, from the chief priests and the elders of the people. Now the betrayer had given them a sign, saying, 'The one I shall kiss is the man; seize him.' And he came up to Jesus at once and said, 'Hail, Master!' And he kissed him. Jesus said to him, 'Friend, why are you here?' Then they came up and laid hands on Jesus and seized him. And behold, one of those who were with Jesus stretched out his hand and drew his sword, and struck the slave of the high priest, and cut off his ear. Then Jesus said to him, "Put your sword back into its place; for all who take the sword will perish by the sword. Do you think that I cannot appeal to my Father and he will at once send me more*

*than twelve legions of angels? But how then should the scriptures be fulfilled that it must be so?' At that hour Jesus said to the crowds, 'Have you come out as against a robber, with swords and clubs to capture me? Day after day I sat in the temple teaching, and you did not seize me. But all this has taken place, that the scriptures of the prophets might be fulfilled.' Then all the disciples forsook him and fled."* (Matthew 26:47-56)

Have students paraphrase the passage. If they have trouble, prompt them with the following questions:

- Why is it significant that Judas betrayed Jesus with a kiss?

- Why does the disciple cut off the ear of the high priest's slave?

- Jesus rebukes the disciple for "defending" him. Why doesn't Jesus fight back or give credit to those who try to stand up for him?

## Discussion

It may make you, as the educator, uncomfortable to come down so hard on Peter in this chapter. Peter has always been portrayed as the shining pillar of the church. This is why it is so essential to read the text and understand what it is actually saying. It is vital that our students understand that we are not to put ourselves above others and that no one is good but God. Set aside any preconceived notions you may be struggling with and allow yourself to learn a different perception alongside the children. Talk with students about potential discomfort with how Peter is actually portrayed and how it differs from how he is talked about today. It is okay to ask questions and observe these differences. Do not, however, fall into the trap of assuming that Peter's rise to saint status means that even if we are sinners, we can become saints too! That is not what this means at all. We can do nothing good. God, on the other hand, is perfectly capable of taking something imperfect and using it for his glory.

Throughout the Bible, a kiss marks a sign of respect and loyalty. The fact that Judas uses a kiss to betray Jesus completely undermines its purpose and meaning. In this passage, the kiss of Judas is lip-service. Judas does and says all the right things (kisses Jesus, calls him Master, etc.), but it means nothing. Jesus himself said earlier in Matthew: "Not everyone who says to me, 'Lord, Lord,' shall enter the kingdom of heaven, but he who does the will of my Father who is in heaven." (Matthew 7:21) Judas' words may be correct, but his actions do not correspond.

An unnamed disciple tries to take action by cutting off the ear of the high priest's slave. In the gospel of John, this disciple is Peter (John 18:10-11). This is unsurprising, given Peter's constant inability to understand what Jesus says. But what is interesting is that Peter cuts off the *ear* of a slave. Not his hand, not his arm, not his leg, but his *ear*. Throughout the gospel, Jesus has been teaching the people with his voice—the only way people can learn is through hearing. The expression "hear the word of the Lord," is a technical phrase from the Old Testament. Now, one of the twelve, who has been charged with preaching the gospel to the poor, has instead taken up the sword (itself a betrayal of Jesus' teaching) in order to cut off the means by which this teaching is received. In a direct betrayal of the Lord's commandment, Peter prevents a slave from hearing the gospel teaching!

Jesus rebukes Peter for his worldly "heroism". Does Peter seriously believe that Jesus needs Peter to defend him? Once again, Peter's lack of faith and self-centered behavior are emphasized. He feels the need to brandish a sword for Jesus when Jesus could easily ask God to send "twelve legions of angels" and be done with this whole business. Peter's defense has nothing to with actually coming to Jesus' aid as much as it has to do with thrusting himself into the limelight. When we come to the aid of others, what are our true motives? Do we really wish to help or do we hope to bring ourselves into focus? Look at what a great guy I am, Peter's actions say. I'm trying to protect Jesus. God does not need anything from man, except to do his will, which Peter has now betrayed.

- Talk with students about questioning their motives when they are moved to help someone. Does that person really need their help? Or is it just to make themselves look good?

- It's evident that Peter is unable to grasp the concept of submission unto death. In Matthew, Jesus is not fighting back because he answers to and obeys the will of his Father.

- Talk with students about what it means to not fight back. What does that look like in their lives?

## Lesson: Matthew 26:57-68

*"Then those who had seized Jesus led him to Ca'iaphas the high priest, where the scribes and the elders had gathered. But Peter followed him at a distance, as far as the courtyard of the high priest, and going inside he sat with the guards to see the end. Now the chief priests and the whole council sought false testimony against Jesus that they might put him to death, but they found none, though many false witnesses came forward. At last two came forward and said, 'This fellow said, "I am able to destroy the temple of God, and to build it in three days." And the high priest stood up and said, 'Have you no answer to make? What is it that these men testify against you?' But Jesus was silent. And the high priest said to him, 'I adjure you by the living God, tell us if you are the Christ, the Son of God.' Jesus said to him, 'You have*

*said so. But I tell you, hereafter you will see the Son of man seated at the right hand of Power, and coming on the clouds of heaven.' Then the high priest tore his robes, and said, 'He has uttered blasphemy. Why do we still need witnesses? You have now heard his blasphemy. What is your judgment?' They answered, 'He deserves death.' Then they spat in his face, and struck him; and some slapped him, saying, 'Prophesy to us, you Christ! Who is it that struck you?'"* (Matthew 26: 57-68)

Have students summarize the passage in their own words. If they have trouble, prompt them with the following questions:

- Who was Ca'iaphas?

- What did the two false witnesses testify against Jesus?

- Jesus said earlier in the gospel that the Temple would be destroyed and he would rebuild it in three days. Ask the students what was meant by this imagery.

- What does the phrase "the Son of man" mean? Where does it come from?

## Discussion

Ask students if they have ever been falsely accused or if they have ever falsely accused others, even if only by refusing to speak up in the person's defense.

Ca'iaphas was the high priest, the son-in-law of Annas. Annas had also served as high priest before being deposed by the Roman emperor. Ca'iaphas' name has been translated as meaning "depression" or "searcher". This is interesting because depression and searching are terms that are often connected. People who suffer from depression are often searching for some greater meaning in their lives. While depression may stem from a chemical imbalance, it causes a level of self-involvement that prevents its sufferers from seeing beyond themselves.

## Lesson: Matthew 26:69-75

*"Now Peter was sitting outside in the courtyard. And a maid came up to him, and said, 'You also were with Jesus the Galilean.' But he denied it before them all, saying, 'I do not know what you mean.' And when he went out to the porch, another maid saw him, and she said to the bystanders, 'This man was with Jesus of Nazareth.' And again he denied it with an oath, 'I do not know the man.' After a little while, the bystanders came up and said to Peter, 'Certainly you are also one of them, for your accent betrays you.' Then he began to invoke a curse on himself and to swear, 'I do not know the man.'" And immediately the cock crowed.*

*And Peter remembered the saying of Jesus, 'Before the cock crows, you will deny me three times.' And he went out and wept bitterly." (Matthew 26: 69-75)*

Have students summarize the passage. If they have trouble, prompt them with the following questions:

- What is Peter doing in the courtyard?

- What is his response to the people who ask him if he was with Jesus?

- Is there significance to the cock as the chosen animal for this passage?

**Discussion**

Peter's name (Cephas) means "stone". Earlier in Matthew, Jesus says, "And I tell you, you are Peter, and on this rock I will build my church, and the powers of death shall not prevail against it" (Matthew 16: 18). The common assumption here is that Peter is a strong cornerstone and foundation of the church. However, another perspective is that Peter is as dense as a rock, but God is able to build the church in spite of him. It's not Peter who builds the church. A rock can do nothing but sit where it is placed. God is taking the dumb, useless thing and turning it into something useful. Peter is like the seed sown among the rocks in the parable of the sower:

*"As for what was sown on rocky ground, this is he who hears the word and immediately receives it with joy; yet he has no root in himself, but endures for a while, and when tribulation or persecution arises on account of the word, immediately he falls away." (Matthew 13: 20-21)*

Talk about how Peter gets excited about the gospel in the beginning. He swears his loyalty to Jesus and the teaching but when he is put to the test, he betrays them both. He likes what Jesus has to say but not enough to truly put his life on the line for it. While Jesus is interrogated, Peter is hanging out in the courtyard. He's sitting. In other gospels, he is "warming himself" (Mark 14:67; Luke 22:55; John 18: 25). Peter is taking care of himself. He's relaxing with the enemies who are questioning his friend. Ask teens if they've ever been really excited about something and then not followed through on it. A common complaint about the millennial generation is that they want to do something meaningful but don't understand the hard work that goes into that kind of life. Talk with students about living in a culture of instant gratification and what it means to pursue a life of purpose.

The mention of the number three here is important. Three is condemnatory in this context because it seals the completeness of Peter's betrayal. After the third time, there are no more chances and the Lord's judgment is at hand, like when a mom warns a child who is delaying carrying out her orders: one, two, three...

The mention of Peter's accent is to mock him. Peter is trying to fit in with the crowd and his accent is embarrassing to him. He is ashamed of his affiliation with Jesus. He pretends he never heard the teaching.

The chicken was not mentioned in the Old Testament. Historians presume that this is because at the time of its writing, there was no such thing as domesticated fowl. Chickens were imported from China, Greece, and Italy into Palestine at a later date than the time of the Old Testament, but early enough to have become common by the time of Jesus' ministry. The cock was noted for its regularity in keeping time. It crowed three times a night: once at half past eleven, again at half past one, and finally at dawn.

## Lesson: Matthew 27:1-10

*"When morning came, all the chief priests and the elders of the people took counsel against Jesus to put him to death; and they bound him and led him away and delivered him to Pilate the governor.*

*"When Judas, his betrayer, saw that he was condemned, he repented and brought back the thirty pieces of silver to the chief priests and the elders, saying, 'I have sinned in betraying innocent blood.' They said, 'What is that to us? See to it yourself.' And throwing down the pieces of silver in the temple, he departed; and he went and hanged himself. But the*

*chief priests, taking the pieces of silver, said, 'It is not lawful to put them into the treasury, since they are blood money.' So they took counsel, and bought with them the potter's field, to bury strangers in. Therefore that field has been called the Field of Blood to this day. Then was fulfilled what had been spoken by the prophet Jeremiah, saying, 'And they took the thirty pieces of silver, the price of him on whom a price had been set by some of the sons of Israel, and they gave them for the potter's field, as the Lord directed me.'"*
*(Matthew 27: 1-10)*

Have students put the passage into their own words. If they have trouble, prompt them with the following questions:

- What did Judas do after he saw that Jesus was condemned?

- Why wouldn't the chief priests put the money in the treasury?

## Discussion

Whenever anyone mentions betrayal in the Bible, Judas is the first name that comes to mind. In fact, the name Judas is so commonly associated with betrayal that our modern English dictionary defines the name "Judas" as "one who betrays under the guise of friendship". We hide from the truth of our own betrayal by accusing Judas and excusing Peter. Which is worse? Betraying your friend into the hands of the enemy or refusing to acknowledge him even after you've given up your whole life to follow him all over the country? The issue is not which betrayal is worse but the fact that it happened at all. We let Peter (and ourselves) off the hook by saying, "He wept bitterly" so he repented. It's okay". But Judas not only repented, he went back and returned the money and even hanged himself. Both men repented, so why do we say that Judas got what he deserved but Peter can go about his business free from judgment? Modern day Christians measure betrayal in degrees, as though one level is worse than the other. We measure sin in the same way. Lying to your parents is not on the same level as murdering a fellow human being. We like to measure sin this way because it allows us to feel superior to someone else. Perhaps we tell lies to our spouse about having an affair, but we tell ourselves that there is no harm...at least we're not killing anyone. In Scripture, all sin is the same. We are all unrighteous. "No one is good but God."

## Lesson: Matthew 27: 11-14

*"Now Jesus stood before the governor; and the governor asked him, 'Are you the King of the Jews?' Jesus said, 'You have said so.' But when he was accused by the chief priests and elders, he made no answer. Then Pilate said to him, 'Do you not hear how many things they testify against you?' But he gave him no answer, not even to a single charge; so that the governor wondered greatly."* (Matthew 27:11-14)

Have students put the passage into their own words. If needed, prompt them with the following questions:

- Why does Jesus make no answer?

- How does Jesus' behavior differ from some others in the Bible who have suffered (e.g. Job)?

## *Discussion*

Here Jesus stands before Pilate and says nothing in his own defense. In a culture of lawsuits over spilled coffee and assertions of individual rights, this makes no sense. Why does Jesus not respond? He is obeying the will of God even unto death. He trusts that God's will supersedes both his human wants and the authority of the human court. He will continue to trust his Father regardless of the consequences for himself.

In the recent children's film "Ferdinand" (based on the book by Munro Leaf), Ferdinand refuses to fight. Even though the matador has his sword drawn and is prepared to kill him, even though Ferdinand could have easily killed El Primero, he refused to fight. In the movie, Ferdinand is staying true to who he is as an individual. In the Bible, Jesus is obeying his Father in heaven. It is the Father who is in control at all times. *Jesus does not answer to Pilate*, he answers *only* to his Father. If he were to answer a Roman authority, he would be acknowledging a human court, which St. Paul condemns in 1 Corinthians.

Talk with teens about what it means to not defend themselves. When a teacher gives them a bad grade, do they defend themselves? When their parents ground them for something they did wrong, do they defend themselves? What does this look like in the bigger picture of today's world?

Offer students a comparison: the contrast between Jesus' attitude towards suffering and the attitude of someone like Job. Job spends over forty chapters complaining about how he is a good man and he doesn't deserve all of the bad things that are happening to him. When Jesus stands before Pilate, he doesn't say to him, "I'm a good guy—you shouldn't be doing this to me. I did everything God said to do. Why is this happening to me?" Jesus simply accepts his situation even though he knows he is going to die. He's already asked God once if he could get out of it but acknowledged that it wasn't about what he wanted. He would do the will of his Father no matter what. Where Job complains, Jesus gets the job done. Discuss with teens whether or not the "why" is as important as obedience.

## Lesson: Matthew 27: 15-26

*"Now at the feast the governor was accustomed to release for the crowd any one prisoner whom they wanted. And they had then a notorious prisoner, called Barab'bas. So when they had gathered, Pilate said to them, 'Whom do you want me to release for*

*you, Barab'bas or Jesus who is called Christ?' For he knew that it was out of envy that they had delivered him up. Besides, while he was sitting on the judgment seat, his wife sent word to him, 'Have nothing to do with that righteous man, for I have suffered much over him today in a dream.' Now the chief priests and the elders persuaded the people to ask for Barab'bas and destroy Jesus. The governor again said to them, 'Which of the two do you want me to release for you?' And they said, 'Barab'bas.' Pilate said tot hem, 'Then whul shall I do with Jesus who is called Christ?' They all said, 'Let him be crucified.' And he said, 'Why, what evil has he done?' But they shouted all the more, 'Let him be crucified.*

*"So when Pilate saw that he was gaining nothing, but rather that a riot was beginning, he took water and washed his hands before the crowd, saying, 'I am innocent of this man's blood; see to it yourselves.' And all of the people answered, 'His blood be on us and on our children!' Then he released for them Barab'bas, and having scourged Jesus, delivered him to be crucified." (Matthew 27:15-26)*

Have students summarize the passage. If they have trouble, prompt them with the following questions:

- What was the custom at the feast?

- What did Pilate ask the crowd?

- What did Pilate's wife have to say?

- Why did Pilate wash his hands?

## Discussion

In Deuteronomy, the people are instructed to wash their hands as a symbolic gesture of being innocent of a slain man's blood. Modern interpretations of Scripture portray Jesus as the rebel who is breaking all the laws. The Pharisees are shown as people who are rigidly following the laws of Moses. The irony is that the opposite is true. In Exodus, the Law is given to Moses by God explicitly saying, "You shall not kill...You shall not bear false witness against your neighbor." (Exodus 20: 13, 16). "Keep far from a false charge, and do not slay the innocent and righteous, for I will not acquit the wicked." (Exodus 23:7) Exodus introduces laws that protect the stranger and the innocent. The Pharisees are not following these laws and Jesus is there to call them back to what God originally commanded. Jesus is not breaking the laws—he is upholding them. It shows how far Israel has strayed in this scene. They have forgotten what God instructed them to do in the Torah. Not only have they forgotten, but they themselves are the very same people that Jesus has repeatedly helped.

People are easily misled and prone to violence. Talk with teens about modern-day Internet mobs, where people are "crucified" on social media. Even Pilate is not immune to the mob's power. Despite his recognition of Jesus' innocence, he hands him over to the crowd to be crucified.

The only person in this passage who is not trying to get the crowd to do what he wants is the person with the most to lose.

## Lesson: Matthew 27:27-37

*"Then the soldiers of the governor took Jesus into the praetorium, and they gathered the whole battalion before him. And they stripped him and put a scarlet robe upon him, and plaiting a crown of thorns they put it on his head, and put a reed in his right hand. And kneeling before him they mocked him, saying, 'Hail, King of the Jews!' And they spat upon him, and took the reed and struck him on the head. And when they had mocked him, they stripped him of the robe, and put his own clothes on him, and led him away to crucify him.*

*"As they went out, they came upon a man of Cyre'ne, Simon by name; this man they compelled to carry his cross. And when they came to a place called Gol'gotha (which means the place of a skull), they offered him wine to drink, mingled with gall; but when he tasted it, he would not drink it. And when they had crucified him, they divided his garments among them by casting lots; then they sat down and kept watch over him there. And over his head they put the charge against him, which read, 'This is Jesus the King of the Jews'." (Matthew 27:27-37)*

Have students summarize the passage. If they have trouble, prompt them with the following questions:

- What is a praetorium?

- What did they do to Jesus when the battalion had gathered?

- What did they say to him?

- Who did they compel to carry the cross?

- What does Gol'gotha mean?

- What did they offer Jesus to drink?

- How did the soldiers dispose of Jesus' clothing?

## Discussion

It is interesting in this passage that the soldiers Jesus admired in previous passages are the ones who torment and torture him. The very thing that connects them—obedience to orders—is the thing that brings them together here. Both are carrying out orders. So too is Simon, who is "compelled" to carry Jesus' cross. Throughout the gospel, Jesus tells people to take up their cross and follow him. This commandment, like any military directive, is not optional. Simon, representative of Israel (the one who "hears") is forced not only to "hear" but to obey the Lord—"compelled" by his Roman enemies, the very people who now persecute Jesus. As in the Old Testament, God co-opts the power of Israel's enemies as an implement of instruction.

## Lesson: Matthew 27:38-66

*"Then two robbers were crucified with him, one on the right and one on the left. And those who passed by derided him, wagging their heads and saying, 'You who would destroy the temple and build it in three days, save yourself! If you are the Son of God, come down from the cross.' So also the chief priests, with the scribes and elders, mocked him, saying, 'He saved others; he cannot save himself. He is the King of Israel; let him come down now from the cross, and we will believe in him. He trusts in God; let God deliver him now, if he desires him; for he said, 'I am the Son*

*of God.' And the robbers who were crucified with him also reviled him in the same way." (Matthew 27:38-44)*

Have students put the passage into their own words. If they struggle, prompt them with the following questions:

- Who was crucified alongside Jesus?

- What did the passersby, the chief priests, scribes, and elder say to him?

- How did the robbers respond?

## Discussion

Here the author makes it a point to note that two robbers are crucified with Jesus on the right and on the left. Earlier in Matthew, the mother of the sons of Zeb'edee asked for her two sons to sit at the Lord's right and left hand in his kingdom (Matthew 20:20-23). They swear that they are able to drink the cup that Jesus drinks and yet when the hour comes, they are nowhere to be found. No one is bickering about who gets to sit at Jesus' right and left now. He is the subject of mockery from people who are still looking for a worldly hero and big, flashy miracles. Even the robbers revile Jesus. The absence of James and John after their big talk is just as bad, perhaps even worse, than the behavior of those who are making fun of him. It is one thing for a stranger to mock you, but another for a friend to abandon you. Again, it is a betrayal. The question, "Is it I," looms large throughout.

## Lesson: Matthew 27:45-50

*"Now from the sixth hour there was darkness over all the land until the ninth hour. And about the ninth hour Jesus cried with a loud voice, "Eli, Eli, la'ma sabach-tha'ni?" that is, 'My God, my God, why has thou forsaken me?' And some of the bystanders hearing it said, 'This man is calling Eli'jah.' And one of them at once ran and took a sponge, filled it with vinegar, and put it on a reed, and gave it to him to drink. But the others said, 'Wait, let us see whether Eli'jah will come to save him.' And Jesus cried again with a loud voice and yielded up his spirit."* (Matthew 27:45-50)

Have students summarize the passage. If necessary, prompt them with the following questions:

- What happened at the sixth hour?

- What happened at the ninth hour?

- What did the bystanders have to say about what Jesus said?

## *Discussion*

Jesus is calling out the title of Psalm 22. While some might suggest that this means the Old Testament predicted

Jesus, it makes more sense that Jesus is referring back to the Old Testament. His entire life has been devoted to its teaching and he demonstrates this by quoting it from the Cross, with his last breath! Then he dies. His job is finished. He has taught the word of God to the people. Still, the people are still waiting for some kind of miracle. They want to see if Eli'jah will come down in his fiery chariot to save the day (2 Kings 2:11). They don't want to face Jesus' defeat. It's embarrassing to have a guy who doesn't defend himself and allows himself to be killed as your king. In worldly terms, that isn't how things are done. Nobody would elect a president whose military policy is to give up the country to the enemy. Ask the children to imagine what the world would be like if kings and presidents chose to lose rather than fight? What would it be like if the children themselves refused to fight with their siblings?

## Lesson: Matthew 27:51-61

*"And behold, the curtain of the temple was torn in two, from top to bottom; and the earth shook, and the rocks were split; the tombs also were opened, and many bodies of the saints who had fallen asleep were raised, and coming out of the tombs after his resurrection they went into the holy city and appeared to many. When the centurion and those who were with him, keeping watch over Jesus, saw the earthquake and what took place, they were filled with*

awe, and said, 'Truly this was the Son of God!' There were also many women there, looking on from afar, who had followed Jesus from Galilee, ministering to him; among whom were Mary Mag'dalene, and Mary the mother of James and Joseph, and the mother of the sons of Zeb'edee.

"When it was evening, there came a rich man from Arimathe'a, named Joseph, who also was a disciple of Jesus. He went to Pilate and asked for the body of Jesus. Then Pilate ordered it to be given to him. And Joseph took the body, and wrapped it in a clean linen shroud, and laid it in his own new tomb, which he had hewn in the rock; and he rolled a great stone to the door of the tomb, and departed. Mary Mag'dalene and the other Mary were there, sitting opposite the sepulchre." (Matthew 27: 51-61)

Have students summarize the passage. If necessary, prompt them with the following questions:

- What is the significance of the curtain of the temple being torn in two?

- Why were the women standing off at a distance?

- Joseph, a rich man from Arimathe'a, takes the body of Jesus and puts it in a tomb. Why?

## Discussion

The curtain of the temple separated God's teaching from the people. Only the high priest was allowed to go into the "Holy of Holies". The rending of the curtain declared that the peoples of the earth were no longer separated from God and that the barrier between Jew and Gentile was erased. The Torah is no longer held back by the Temple. God favors all the peoples of the earth. All are his children.

The women hanging around at a distance from where Jesus was are often interpreted as the only ones who stood by Jesus until death, yet this is not the case. They are also standing afar off so as not to be associated with their embarrassing teacher, who hangs from a cross in shame:

> *"And if a man has committed a crime punishable by death and he is put to death, and you hang him on a tree, his body shall not remain all night upon the tree, but you shall bury him the same day, for a hanged man is accursed by God; you shall not defile your land which the Lord your God gives you for an inheritance. " (Deuteronomy 22:22-23)*

It is important to consider this passage from Deuteronomy when discussing Joseph of Arimathe'a. In most Biblical commentaries, Joseph is seen as doing something nice for Jesus by taking his body and putting it in an expensive tomb made of stone. However, Joseph takes Jesus down and puts him in a tomb of rock. If he was truly Jesus' disciple, wouldn't he be waiting for the Resurrection? Instead, Joseph buries Jesus, puts a big stone in front of the door, and leaves. He takes Jesus down so he will not be left upon the cross all night. A "hanged man is accursed by God" and the land cannot be defiled. What Joseph's actions imply is that although he was a disciple of Jesus (according to Matthew), he didn't really trust in the Lord's promise. In Mark, Joseph was a "respected member of the council"—the same council that decided to put Jesus to death (Mark 15:42-47). The women who are now by the tomb don't really trust either because they did nothing to stop Joseph from shutting Jesus up in the tomb—from hiding him away to avoid the shame of his defeat.

## Lesson: Matthew 27:62-66

*"Next day, that is, after the day of Preparation, the chief priests and the Pharisees gathered before Pilate and said, "Sir, we remember how that impostor said, while he was still alive, 'After three days I will rise again.' Therefore order the sepulchre to be made secure until the third day, lest his disciples go and steal him away, and tell the people, 'He has risen from the dead,' and the last fraud will be worse than the first.' Pilate said to them, 'You have a guard of soldiers; go, make it as secure as you can.' So they went and made the sepulchre secure by sealing the stone and setting a guard." (Matthew 27: 62-66)*

Have students summarize the passage. If necessary, prompt them with the following questions:

- What happened after the day of Preparation?

- What did the chief priests and Pharisees want?

- How did Pilate respond?

## Discussion

Once again, the intent is to control the situation and ensure that Jesus is actually dead. But nothing, not the Temple, not a tomb of stone, not a Roman guard—nothing—will keep Jesus from fulfilling the mission assigned by his Father. The curtain has been torn, the tomb will open, and the Torah will be preached to all nations.

## Lesson: Matthew 28:1-15

*"Now after the sabbath, toward the dawn of the first day of the week, Mary Mag'dalene and the other Mary went to see the sepulchre. And behold, there was a great earthquake; for an angel of the Lord descended from heaven and came and rolled back the stone, and sat upon it. His appearance was like lightning, and his raiment white as snow. And for fear of him the guards trembled and became like dead men. But the*

*angel said to the women, 'Do not be afraid; for I know that you seek Jesus who was crucified. He is not here; for he has risen, as he said. Come, see the place where he lay. Then go quickly and tell his disciples that he has risen from the dead, and behold, he is going before you to Galilee; there you will see him. Lo, I have told you. So they departed quickly from the tomb with fear and great joy, and ran to tell his disciples. And behold, Jesus met them and said, 'Hail!' And they came up and took hold of his feet and worshiped him. Then Jesus said to them, 'Do not be afraid; go and tell my brethren to go to Galilee, and there they will see me.'" (Matthew 28: 1-10)*

Have students summarize the passage. If necessary, prompt them with the following questions:

- Who went to see the Sepulcher?

- What happened when the women arrived?

- What did the angel say to the women?

- When they left the tomb, who did they meet?

## Discussion

Mary Mag'dalene and the other Mary have come to see the Sepulcher. What is interesting about the Resurrection is that Jesus still does not put on a show. The big earthquakes always happen when he is not around, keeping the focus on the Father's power. When the women run into him on the road, it is an arbitrary meeting. Jesus greets them with "Hail!" like it's no big deal. Then Jesus tells them to go ahead into Galilee, where the gospel is to be preached to the nations. The mission must be fulfilled!

## Lesson: Matthew 28:11-15

*"While they were going, behold, some of the guard went into the city and told the chief priests all that had taken place. And when they had assembled with the elders and taken counsel, they gave a sum of money to the soldiers and said, 'Tell people, "His disciples came by night and stole him away while we were asleep." And if this comes to the governor's ears, we will satisfy him and keep you out of trouble.' So they took the money and did as they were directed; and this story has been spread among the Jews to this day." (Matthew 28:11-15)*

Have students summarize the passage. If necessary, prompt them with the following questions:

- Who did the guards go to see?

- What did the chief priests and elders do about it?

## Discussion

Even after everything that has happened, even after the testimony of the guards, the chief priests are still trying to control the narrative. They bribe the soldiers with money and give them a version of events to tell everyone; promising to keep them out of trouble. Instead of spreading the teaching of God, they abuse their power to spread self-serving lies.

## Lesson: Matthew 28:16-20

*"Now the eleven disciples went to Galilee, to the mountain to which Jesus had directed them. And when they saw him they worshiped him; but some doubted. And Jesus came and said to them, 'All authority in heaven and on earth has been given to me. Go therefore and make disciples of all nations, baptizing them in the name of the Father and of the Son and of the Holy Spirit, teaching them to observe all that I have commanded you; and lo, I am with you always, to the close of the age. (Matthew 28:16-20)*

Have students summarize the passage. If necessary, prompt them with the following questions:

- Where did the disciples go?

- What happened when they got there?

- What did Jesus command them to do?

## Discussion

Students may wonder which mountain the disciples were
directed to. There is no specific mountain named here—
some commentators believe it was Mt. Tabor; some feel it
was the mountain where the Beatitudes were preached.
But it is evident that the exact location is not important,
otherwise the author would have identified it. However,
the terrain *is* significant. The fact that they are sent back
to the mountain brings to mind Jesus' earlier comment
that if one has "faith as a grain of mustard seed, you will
say to this mountain, 'Move from here to there' and it will
move; and nothing will be impossible to you" (Matthew
17:20). By faith, the mountain of Exodus is moved from
Sinai to Galilee of the nations. The impossible has
happened. The law of Moses is now available to all.

When the disciples finally get to see Jesus, Matthew
emphasizes that there are now only eleven—they have
lost one along the way. Humans are stubborn; even when
they see Jesus in person, some disciples doubt. It becomes
clear why Jesus wasn't a fan of miracles. Even when
people see the incredible, they still do not believe. It is the
hearing of the commandment, not seeing, that Jesus
desires. Thus, Jesus *commands* them to go out to all the
nations and *teach*, reminding them that he is with them
always. Some may take that as a nice sentiment...oh, Jesus
is still with us, isn't that great? But it's more of a warning:
"I am with you through my words. I have my eye on you.

Keep my commandments. Don't screw up. Keep teaching
Scripture!"

# Epilogue: On Parenting

The study of the Bible, like parenting, is not an easy task. "Experts" offer many interpretations of the "how" or the "why" of parenting in an endless selection of books. This leaves one feeling bewildered and inadequate. When I first became a mother, I hunted for the perfect Orthodox parenting book that would teach me everything I needed to know. At the time, there was not much available. Today, if you browse online searches, you will find countless opinions about how to raise children in the Orthodox faith. Blogs suggest turning homes into monasteries where children pray several times a day. In Orthodox social media groups, mothers post pictures of their kids saying prayers, lighting candles, or pretending to be in church. Some parents look for toys that mimic church items. Parenting advice is constantly sought out on how to get children to love church. Responses typically revolve around fasting or getting kids to church services or the kinds of prayers to say for your children.

Many of these things can be helpful, but they are not primary. By themselves, they cannot equip our children to live in the world. Worse, they often focus on keeping kids in church for *our* benefit. It is the Bible that exposes our hypocrisy as teachers and parents. It is the Bible that is the *essential* source that gives meaning to our traditions and validity to our practices. The most beautiful thing about our church is that people can't give their opinion or make up their own prayers. We have formal prayers that conform to the content of the Bible. As I attempted to maintain an "Orthodox hipster" lifestyle, I quickly realized it would fail me because there was no substance. Little did I know that the book that would help me the most was collecting dust on my bookshelf.

Someone once asked in an Orthodox parenting Facebook group what books they should read to their children. The caveat, of course, was that the books had to be "Orthodox" or "Christian" in nature. Not a single person recommended the Bible. Stories of saints were the most popular, followed by books about monks or nuns and prayers. Again, these things are valuable, but they do not make up the core of our faith. They do not challenge our children with the source of all wisdom, let alone offer substance for critical thinking. When our children are older, picture books and Sunday school curricula will not suffice for the problems they will face in the world—the very real problems the Bible tackles head on: violence, abuse, greed, cruelty, elitism, exceptionalism, entitlement, the victim mentality, self-righteousness, materialism, egoism, and the lust for power, to name a few.

It is our duty as parents to give our children the light for dark places and to trust that God will show them when and how to use it. Do not let your inner drive for perfection get in the way of the good. Fear cannot be a deterrent for doing God's work. The work God desires will never be done to his standard because we are human and incapable of reaching his level. But if we don't teach our children the Bible because we are afraid of teaching imperfectly, then it is about our own ego and not about our children. Kids will benefit more from a botched attempt than they will from no attempt at all. If our children's salvation depends on our skills and personal wisdom as teachers, then they are doomed.

It is not our duty to save our children, it is our duty to teach our children. Their salvation is in God's hands. While this handing over of complete control to God is terrifying, it is also liberating. The pressure the modern church exerts to "save" or "retain" our children can be debilitating. They are less concerned about salvation than they are about numbers...which translates to donations for expensive buildings. Talking about church growth is another way of talking about money. This duplicity combined with the lack of critical thinking and Biblical instruction for our children is why the Orthodox church struggles to retain its youth. Children can smell hypocrisy and their correct instinct is to flee.

In an attempt to tighten their grip, the solution that most Orthodox (indeed, most Christians) choose for their children is separation and social isolation. Ironically, the text most commonly cited to justify this separation is John 15:18-19:

> *"If the world hates you, know that it has hated me before it hated you. If you were of the world, the world would*

*love its own; but because you are not of the world, but I*
*chose you out of the world, therefore the world hates you."*

Christians use this verse as a defense for almost everything. It gives them an excuse to make victims of themselves and of their children. This is incorrect. Exchanging "Merry Christmas" for "Happy Holidays" is not persecution. Your neighbor's inability to comprehend your refusal to participate in Halloween is not persecution. The media's scathing reports on the political hero of your choice is not persecution. John's gospel was written to encourage the faithful in the aftermath of persecution and mass persecution that frequently resulted in martyrdom. This verse was written as an encouragement to the faithful to "remember that persecution is to be expected" and "if Jesus is their Lord, they must be prepared to endure the same sufferings he did".[1] What is discussed here is actual physical torture and suffering, not civil laws or political ideologies that conflict with our views. A law that does not conform with our political, religious or moral views does not count as persecution.

Paul reminds us in Romans 12:2 that we are not to be *"conformed to this world: but be ye transformed by the renewing of your mind, that ye may prove what that is good, acceptable, and perfect, will of God."* He is not talking about our dress code or personal identity or customs. He is

---

[1] Paul Nadim Tarazi, *The New Testament: Introduction, vol 3, Johannine Writings,* (Crestwood, New York: SVS Press, 1999).

talking about our way of acting and thinking. He is not telling us to create our own religious state. We are commanded to associate with the unbelievers, yet this doesn't mean to approach them with a savior complex. By pretending that unbelievers are out to get the good, honest, hardworking Christians of the world, we create an "us" *vs.* "them" mentality that is not Scriptural. People who base their faith around dress codes, fasting, and segregation based on rigid theology have simply created a new Caesar. They are not worshiping God, they are worshiping their own piety. We were not commanded to separate. We were commanded to embrace our neighbor as well as the stranger and sojourner. It is God who separates one from another through his commandment, and only he can judge.

In this way, the Bible is our guide to being in the world but not of it. The Bible is the only access we have to God's will for us. Without it, we have nothing. We are repeatedly commanded to love the stranger and the sojourner. Yet through misguided interpretation and ideology, we have moved away from God's commandment. We use the Bible for our Christian consumerism, asking, "what can it do for us", rather than, "what is it teaching us to do?" If we don't get out of it what we think we should be getting, we put it on the shelf and read the canons and the church fathers instead. We offer our children opinions of the text instead of the text itself and expect that to be enough. Then we are shocked when they go off to find their own personal Caesar—one that agrees with their view of the world.

Faced with this reality, the educator may feel that even attempting to teach the Bible to children is futile. Don't be discouraged. Like the parable of the talent, it is better to have tried and failed than to have done nothing at all. Parents must remember that they have no control over their children's salvation. Only God is in control. This is the most important thing that the Bible taught me, namely, that I cannot save my children. I can do everything perfectly and I am still unable to save them (think Job). Teaching your children the Bible will not produce the perfect offspring, but it will equip them with tools to go out and face the world on their own, in obedience to God's will.

*"...Nevertheless not my will, but thine, be done." (Luke 22:42)*

# Helpful Resources

It can be difficult to know where to begin when studying the historical context of the Bible. Your local library is an excellent resource if you know where to look. Search for books on ancient Roman history to understand the type of government people lived under in the New Testament. This history is critical for understanding both the story of Jesus and the writings of Paul. The Internet is also a helpful resource. Below are links to websites and podcasts that I used for the writing of this book, and also refer to often for my own Bible study.

## The Ephesus School Podcast Network

https://ephesusschool.org/

### *The Bible as Literature*

Listen to Fr. Marc Boulos and Dr. Richard Benton discuss the Biblical text every Thursday morning, with an ongoing, verse-by-verse discussion of each book.

### *Tarazi Tuesdays*

Tuesday episodes of *The Bible as Literature* feature Fr. Paul Nadim Tarazi, whose mastery of the Bible and biblical languages is unparalleled.

### Teach Me Thy Statutes

Each week, Fr. Aaron Warwick and Jason Ewertt meet to discuss biblical readings from the Orthodox lectionary.

### Tewahido Bible Study

Dn. Henok Elias of the Ethiopian Orthodox Church offers a weekly examination of the sacred scriptures, with special attention given to the original languages.

## Other Sources

### Ears to Hear

Each week, Fr. Fouad Saba, pastor of St. George Antiochian Orthodox Church in Cicero, Illinois, publishes a wonderful Bible study on YouTube. You can find a link to his program on ephesusschool.org.

### Naked Bible Podcast

http://www.nakedbiblepodcast.com/

Dr. Michael Heisner strips the Biblical text down to the bare essentials—language, etymology, motifs, etc.

### Rediscover Christianity

https://www.dustinlyon.org/

Fr. Dustin Lyon's regular blog posts help his readers unlock the Bible's meaning.

## The Orthodox Center for the Advancement of Biblical Studies

http://www.ocabspress.org/

The Orthodox Center for the Advancement of Biblical Studies (OCABS) was established to educate, inspire and challenge the faithful to recognize the centrality of sound biblical interpretation for life in Christ.

## Bible Study Tools

https://www.biblestudytools.com/

A quick reference guide for Biblical commentaries, texts, dictionaries, etc.

Finally, if you would like to learn more about narration as an educational tool:

## The Complete Writer

https://welltrainedmind.com/

Susan Wise Bauer, the author of *The Well Trained Mind,* offers an excellent writing curriculum centered around narration. If you would like further information on how narration works, this is the series for you.

CPSIA information can be obtained
at www.ICGtesting.com
Printed in the USA
BVHW081423150720
583807BV00005B/240